WITHDRAWN NEWTON FREE LIBRARY
NEWTON, MA

S0-BOL-772

LIVING
THIN

A partnership between American Library Association
and FINRA Investor Education Foundation

FINRA is proud to support the American Library Association

LIVING THIN

One woman's journey from penniless to prosperous in a year

Antonia Magee

Wrightbooks

First published 2010 by Wrightbooks
an imprint of John Wiley & Sons Australia, Ltd
42 McDougall Street, Milton Qld 4064

Office also in Melbourne

Typeset in ITC New Baskerville 11.3/14.3pt

332.024
M27L
2010

© Antonia Magee 2010

The moral rights of the author have been asserted

National Library of Australia Cataloguing-in-Publication entry

Author:	Magee, Antonia.
Title:	Living thin: one woman's journey from penniless to prosperous in a year / Antonia Magee.
ISBN:	9781742169767 (pbk.)
Subjects:	Finance, Personal. Wealth. Financial security.
Dewey Number:	332.024

All rights reserved. Except as permitted under the *Australian Copyright Act 1968* (for example, a fair dealing for the purposes of study, research, criticism or review), no part of this book may be reproduced, stored in a retrieval system, communicated or transmitted in any form or by any means without prior written permission. All inquiries should be made to the publisher at the address above.

Cover design by Qualia Creative

Printed in China by Printplus Limited

10 9 8 7 6 5 4 3 2 1

Disclaimer

The material in this publication is of the nature of general comment only, and does not represent professional advice. It is not intended to provide specific guidance for particular circumstances and it should not be relied on as the basis for any decision to take action or not take action on any matter which it covers. Readers should obtain professional advice where appropriate, before making any such decision. To the maximum extent permitted by law, the author and publisher disclaim all responsibility and liability to any person, arising directly or indirectly from any person taking or not taking action based upon the information in this publication.

This book is a work of fiction. Except as advised below, all people, companies and events in this work are fictional. Certain characters, while inspired by real people in the author's life, have been fictionalised for the purposes of this work. The individuals mentioned do not endorse the views, attitudes or opinions within this book, which are the author's alone.

Jason Cunningham, who is mentioned within this book, is not fictional although certain comments and conversations made by him within the book may be fictionalised. Jason is a practising financial adviser, an author published by John Wiley & Sons Australia Ltd, and has been consulted in the development of this publication.

Contents

Acknowledgements

I was told writers usually acknowledge their parents, their partners and their publishers after completing a book so who am I to argue with history?

Mum and Dad: No daughter could have two better supporters and role models. Thanks for all you love and encouragement.

Mary and Kate: You have both made writing *Living Thin* incredibly easy for me. Your publishing talents astound me and the book would not have been half as good without your awesome editing and guidance.

Jason: What can I say? You are truly a financial guru and the only person to ever have made money make sense to me — no mean feat.

Gilly, Dave and Adso: Geniuses.

My dear siblings and friends: you have all shaped this book in some way and I thank you.

And Steve: Who would have thunk it?? X

Introduction

My name is Maggie Rose and just a little over 12 months ago I was 29, single and perpetually broke. This was something I had needed to address for some time—being broke, that is, not the age or the status. I was in debt and unhappy, and as I watched my friends adapt to life and responsibly deal with problems as they arose, I continued to be the kind of woman who ran headlong into a bad situation until it dragged me to the ground kicking and screaming. I knew something had to give.

I had racked up thousands of dollars in credit card debt, was living pay cheque to pay cheque and had an absolute inability to save money. Unless I figured out a way to manage my funds I could see I was destined for a lifetime of share house living and the age pension—something every woman should be scared of as it doesn't go a long way.

I needed to take stock of my life and I decided that if I was ever going to be a successful saver, I had to go on a serious financial diet and learn to live thin. So, just like going on a diet to lose weight, my plan was to lose debt then, rather than stacking on the weight again via credit cards, I was going to fatten up my bank account to the tune of $10 000.

My job as a journalist doesn't pay a lot, but I was earning enough to sort myself out and, with the help of my friends, a lot of research, DIY lunches and a financial adviser, I set out to achieve my goals in a year.

There were a lot of ups and downs as I had myriad bad habits and a penchant for big nights out with good food, good wine and good friends. I wasn't willing to give up my social life and be miserable just to have some cash in the bank, I wanted to be able to have my cake and eat it too. I just had to learn how to do it on the cheap and exercise restraint.

This all took place as I struggled through an exciting and stressful year at work, and with my love life taking more twists than a semitrailer trying to do a three-point turn in an alley. So to all those women whose finances are out of control, this book is written for you—read on, try living thin and see what a difference it can make.

PART I

Youth, stupidity, whatever you want to call it

1 January to 31 January

Universal credit card: $5500 owing
LAND credit card: $1000 owing
Parking fines: $400
Happiness: quickly turning to panic and guilt

My friend Max used to tell me the last year of a person's 20s was the first stage of their Saturn Return. He said the 29th year was the end of one life cycle and the beginning of another. Saturn Return is the term astrologers use to describe the amount of time the planet Saturn takes to orbit the sun—about 29.5 years. The theory behind the return is when a person is about to reach 30, Saturn has made one orbit around the sun and the transition from youth to adulthood can be made. At the end of the next 29.5-year cycle one would make the transition from adulthood to maturity, and then, finally, assuming you are lucky enough to reach your late 80s, wisdom is bestowed—a long time to wait for enlightenment you'd think.

When Max was in his 30th year he started his own architecture firm and met the love of his life, Jem. He often told me—even though I was a witness to nearly all of it—that it was a year of incredible upheaval. Everything in his life finally fell into place and he said it all linked back to the Saturn Return.

Max was the kind of person who was forever trying to make me feel better when I had either hit the bottom of a relationship, a fling or my bank account. The Saturn Return subject only came up after we'd had a few glasses of red wine and I was waxing lyrical about how depressed I was. Our talks were not frequent, but Max was intuitive enough to know when I needed support.

Max was three years older than me and had been one of my closest friends since our teen years. He first told me about the theory when I started my journalism career. I was 25 years old and the Saturn Return was supposed to be something to look forward to—the point at which I would finally move into true adulthood, accepting all of the accompanying responsibilities, and everything in my life would fall into place. At the time Max had just finished his degree after studying architecture as a mature-age student, while I had finally convinced the editor at *The City* newspaper to take me on as a copygirl because I couldn't get a job as a reporter. After two years I was finally given a job as a journalist.

We were out in the world, single, footloose and fancy free—or Fancy Maggie, as Max used to call me. By about the fourth time I'd heard his theory it was safe to say I could see it coming. But I always felt a glimmer of hope when my head hit the pillow afterwards.

Most people will think the Saturn Return theory is complete and utter rubbish: just turning 30 is upheaval enough. On my 29th birthday Max sat me down and gave me another pep talk. I was heading into my fifth year at the paper and he asked me what I wanted for the future. I told him I was happy at *The City*, but I wanted to be able to support myself. As far as men went, I was not particularly interested in a relationship. Sure, it would have been nice to be in a happy, healthy relationship, but I was not on the prowl for a new man, as I had just got rid of the old one after a little over a year.

When 1 January rolled around and I was officially two months into my 29th year, things hadn't started out so auspiciously. Basically my work ensured I managed to avoid any sort of fun, and I spent the evening on a beach with a photographer colleague watching thousands of teenagers grope one another before their 1.30 am curfews. Each year hundreds of junior reporters the world over are sent to cover New Year's Eve celebrations while the older media types get a night off. It is one of many rites of passage a career as a journalist holds. Some of them are great—I get to see and sometimes be a part of history as it unfolds, meet ordinary people doing the most extraordinary things and, of course, I wouldn't be doing it all if I didn't get to write. But the New Year's thing sucked.

The photographer and I ate dinner together at a local Italian restaurant with the expenses *The City* had sent us to the coast with. Despite our lack of enthusiasm about the night ahead, we made the best of the meal and shared a bottle of red, so it wasn't a complete write-off.

We had been sent to the beach to report on the festivities, but what my boss really wanted was a big fight to break out. New Year's on the coast is notorious for underage teens getting horribly drunk, having sex and getting into brawls. The paper's New Year's Day edition is always peppered with stories of drunken shenanigans. Although I didn't want all hell to break loose, personally I was praying for a story to emerge so my boss would finally give me a break. Nothing particularly newsworthy happened, though; instead, I had to settle for a highly uncomfortable kind of voyeurism and a bottle of beer before bed. My story in the next day's edition was a hack job consisting of near-fights and outrage at the number of underage drinkers. However, to my surprise when I picked up a copy of the New Year's Day paper I realised I'd made it sound like it had been an eventful evening; describing the fireworks in minute detail might have had something to do with it.

The only reprieve the New Year offered was that I got a 24-hour break from staking out the Ponzi scheme mastermind Jack O'Brien—another brilliant junior reporter job that was seemingly assigned to stop me from having a life or progressing my career. It wasn't an unworthy story: O'Brien was the latest scumbag businessman who had siphoned off hundreds of millions of dollars of other people's hard-earned cash—in other words, a real piece of work. He had managed to convince hundreds of investors that their life savings would be better off in his hands. The investors weren't dimwitted; O'Brien had the credentials to get him on the board of any central bank in the G8. However, he wasn't actually investing any money. He was just shuffling it around so the investors thought they were making money in the sharemarket while he was living the life of Riley in his five penthouses. O'Brien was an out-and-out crook who lost honest people's homes, superannuation funds and life savings with seemingly no remorse.

By the time I was on his tail he had been released from jail after serving only two years of a 20-year sentence. He had appealed and had, unbelievably, been let off on a technicality. His first trial was reported with only minor interest, but when the enormity of his crime was eventually revealed the media jumped on the bandwagon and kept the public captivated with up-to-the-minute information on his appeal from their laptops in the courtroom and on the front pages of every metropolitan paper in the country. Spencer Lee, a young-gun reporter from one of *The City*'s rival papers, had broken the story. He had gone on to earn multiple accolades and awards for his work and was a bit of hero around the journalism traps.

I started the stake-out about two weeks before Christmas. My role was basically to sit in a car and watch the door of O'Brien's inner-city apartment building and wait for him to appear. *The City*'s editor said she wanted to get something back for the people who had lost everything. O'Brien may have gotten away with his Ponzi scheme in court, but there was no doubt in anyone's mind he was a criminal, and if he wasn't going to jail, then he was to be made the business equivalent of a Hollywood actor considered box office poison.

I was told the editor wanted an exclusive interview. I don't know how she thought this was going to happen while I was sitting in a car—O'Brien never seemed to leave his home. Well, not that I had seen.

I was desperate to prove myself so I could get off the general beat and convince the powers that be I deserved my own column. O'Brien, although not exactly the kind of job I wanted to be following, kept me out of the office and out of view of Janice Green, my news chief, who had taken a particular disliking to me. Little did I know it would be months before I laid eyes on O'Brien, let alone had a chance to talk to him—I have a feeling Janice did, though.

As a consequence of sitting in a car for weeks, by the time the new year rolled around my back was in such pain I was starting to feel crippled and the lack of exercise was making me feel antsy and fat. The weather was sweltering and if I hadn't had air conditioning and an Otis Redding CD my brain would have melted from boredom.

Apart from my back pain, the heat and the Ponzi swine, I also had a more pressing problem. It was the first of the month, my rent was due and I only had two-thirds of the money in my savings account. I didn't get paid until the following Wednesday, which was still six days away and meant at least part of my rent would be late. I'd been withdrawing cash without checking my account balance for weeks thinking I still had plenty of money to cover the rent. It was only when I went to transfer the funds on 1 January that I realised I was short.

Up until that day I had always paid my rent on time. It was the one thing I made sure I had enough cash to pay. Parking fines and bills could come and go, but I was not going to be kicked out of a house. Christmas, however, had stripped my bank balance and I had no buffer. In the weeks leading up to Christmas Day I distinctly remember feeling optimistic about my finances. There was cash in the bank and some leeway on my two credit cards. But by New Year's Day both cards were bursting at the seams and I was once again waiting for the next pay cheque.

It wasn't as though I had gone over the top buying presents. I had two brothers to buy gifts for, plus my parents. There was no boyfriend to worry about and my friends and I didn't exchange presents. I had spent the money on something; I just couldn't for the life of me think of what it was.

I was already two months into my supposed year of reincarnation and here I was stuck in a stifling car, weighing up whether to wait a week and have enough money to survive the next six days or just transfer what I had, be completely broke and pay the balance later. When I started working at *The City* I thought getting paid weekly was going to solve all my money problems as I had always been paid fortnightly and was close to broke by the start of the second week. I soon realised the weekly pay cheque was no different and I was usually low on funds by the end of the week.

As well as the rent, I also had to consider my best friend Eliza's 30th birthday dinner coming up the following week. In another life I was sure I was the kind of person who paid the rent and gave a polite apology for not turning up to the dinner, or showed a bit of restraint and stuck to a budget. Unfortunately, the New Years' Eve assignment meant that I was now dying for a night out and common sense did not prevail.

I know a normal person would have bypassed all the internal suffering and just paid the bloody rent. Not I. I was a sucker for my own punishment. I liked to keep things pent up inside and let them fester before I finally exploded. In my defence, I never imagined I would be approaching 30 and have nothing to show for over a decade of work. Like most people I just assumed I would have a good job, a healthy savings balance and be getting paid a handsome wage.

In reality I was earning $53 500 a year, but living like I was earning $85 000 — something had to give. I sat in the car for days and looked sadly over my bank statements on the laptop perched on my knees. I couldn't figure out where it had all gone so wrong. There were a lot of purchases at restaurants and bars, but that was hardly surprising considering all the festive dinners I had gone to.

Whichever way I looked at it, my finances were in a sorry state. I had two credit cards: the Universal card was maxed out to its $5500 limit and I was nearing the end of credit on a new LAND credit card with a $1000 limit. I didn't even know how to begin paying either card off. I wanted them gone in one hit and paying off the minimum just didn't seem worth it. I had tried to work out how much interest I was paying on each card, but the layout of the statements was beyond me so I put them with all the other papers stacked on my desk at home.

I was paid $1028 a week before tax and my university loan were taken out. Of this I took home approximately

$772 when I was paid each Wednesday. My general expenses included:

- ✳ $1000 a month on rent
- ✳ $300 a week on going out (taxis, meals, alcohol and the occasional packet of cigarettes)
- ✳ $40 a week on breakfast at a cafe near work
- ✳ $70 a week on supermarket shopping if I happened to be staying in a few nights that week
- ✳ $60 a month gym membership
- ✳ $90 a month for car, home and health insurance
- ✳ $350 a month for my mobile phone and utilities.

My gym membership and the three insurances were all paid via direct debit from my savings account. This meant I usually didn't have to think much about the payments unless one of the debits fell on a day when I had no money in my account and I received a letter from the bank warning me I was going to be fined. Needless to say, from the amount I was spending money was tight.

My car was the only valuable asset I had, apart from a few beloved pieces of furniture that had more sentimental value than anything else. It was a 15-year-old Volvo I had bought when I was 20. It didn't cost that much to keep on the road and, apart from the parking fines that seemed to attach themselves to my windscreen like it was a super-strong magnet, most of the money for the vehicle went on parking and petrol.

If I was ever going to get my act together, my lifestyle and spending habits had to change fast. I had nothing to do but wait for O'Brien to leave his building, so I wrote down a list of things I could and couldn't change. It was a little lopsided but a start nonetheless.

Stay	Go
• Regular haircut and dye	• Going out so often
• Dumpling dinners with Max and Jem	• Credit cards
• Gym membership	• Weekly blow-waves
• Good-quality food	• Driving to work
• Living with Fran and Tim	• Expensive wine (could buy cheaper)
• Books	• Breakfast at work every day
• Weekly swims	• Occasional drunken cigarettes
• Car	

I lived with two friends, Tim and Fran, in a beautiful old house, about three kilometres from the city, that had been renovated within an inch of its life. Rent wasn't cheap, but the house was a stunner. I had longed for a home with central heating and air conditioning after years of living in cold hovels and sharing a bathroom with four other people. Our house had it all, as well as a pool and two bathrooms. The suburb was filled with great bars and galleries, and was close to the river.

Fran had become one of my closest friends while we were at university. She was studying several media subjects as part of her political science degree and we had ended up sitting next to each other in all our tutorials and becoming great mates. She had worked as an adviser to a government minister for five years and just before

Christmas had thrown in the towel and gone to work at a fashion house.

I had inherited Tim as a friend through Fran. They had grown up in the same country town and gone to the same high school. He moved to the city from his parent's wheat farm when he was 16 to train as a chef, and had been working at a swish cafe not far from Jack O'Brien's humble abode since he was 18. The owner, a 30-something French woman called Yvette, had taken a liking to Tim's cheeky ways and taught him everything she knew.

I took a liking to his cheeky ways in the form of a month-long fling when we were about 25. It started and ended with a bang, but after six months of not speaking to one another we discovered we actually got along like a house on fire without having to go to bed. The truth be told, I secretly thought there was something going on with Tim and his boss the whole time anyway.

The three of us had been living together for about 18 months when I randomly decided I could get away with not paying my rent without it having any effect on Fran or Tim. Of course it wasn't something I told them. I guess I thought no-one would notice. For a smart woman, this was one of my most stupid moments.

Looking back and talking about it like this makes it all sound so tawdry. My money situation was bad, but so was plenty of people's. It wasn't like I was some irrational girl who had heart palpitations every time I walked within a 20-kilometre radius of a shoe store. I simply knew no other way to live than from pay cheque to pay cheque. Bills were always paid on time, except parking fines, and I was never out of money for more than a day...two at the most. I had a canny way of spending every cent I earned without going hungry—again something I probably should not have been proud of.

On 10 January, the day of Eliza's birthday party, the rent was 10 days late, even though I had been paid three days earlier. I had started the year with $772, been paid another $772 and still hadn't managed to pay the rent. Instead of going to the real estate agent, the money went towards paying my phone bill, food, going out and a $300 pair of Chanel sunglasses bought on a whim after I tried them on and they looked great, and the lenses were *incredible*. Bad start.

I was in trouble: I wasn't going to get paid again for another four days. I knew I was getting myself into hot water and I can't tell you how much I loathed myself, but I just kept putting it off as though it would all work out in the end. Whoever said karma was going to come around obviously had me in mind. I didn't even help myself by putting money on my credit cards. It all went in one fell swoop—Eliza's birthday.

Eliza's 30th was at Concord's, a wonderful Spanish restaurant she had hired out for 30 of her closest friends and family. I still hadn't heard from our real estate agent and was confident if I paid rent four days after the party, when my next pay cheque arrived, my problems would be solved.

I had met Eliza at high school and we had been friends for close to 20 years. In all that time, give or take a few birthdays when we were in our early teens, we had never bought one another a present. We had made a deal not give each other gifts years before, but I was making an exception for the big 3-0 so I bought her a beautiful handbag.

It was an incredible night. The food and wine were delicious and everyone was making the most of actually getting a table at Concord's and hedonistically splurging. I was seated at a table next to Grace, another good friend who Fran and I had gone to university with. Opposite the two of us were Tim, Max and Jem. Tim's enormous food ego ensured he ordered everything on the menu for the table—quail eggs with truffle cream, prawns, Wagyu beef, jamon and about 20 other tasty morsels. It was magnificent.

As the night wore on and we aptly discussed turning 30, Max asked me if my plans for financial and relationship enlightenment were underway. In the midst of my food and wine happiness I had completely forgotten all about my money problems. I froze and looked guiltily at Tim across the table from me.

'What's wrong, Maggie? You're blushing', Max said.

'No, I'm not, you idiot', I snapped back. 'I've spent the past week stuck in a car alone, so there's not been much of a chance to meet anyone, but everything else is going along nicely.'

'Maggie, I wasn't talking about meeting someone; I meant your dreams of grandeur.'

'I don't think money is polite dinner conversation, Max', I said, desperately attempting to get Max off the subject. He ignored these signs entirely and proceeded to tell all my friends that I had confided my finances were in a spot of bother.

'I did not', I said, blushing again. 'You were telling me about your stupid Saturn Return for the hundredth time and all I said was that I wanted to have financial freedom.'

'Calm down, Maggie. I was just being precocious', he said.

Max then went on to tell our table about the Saturn Return theory and that I had said I was on a mission to get rich and this was the year it was going to happen. These were people I was close to, but I really didn't want them to know just how dire my financial situation was, so I was getting more and more embarrassed as Max went on. When he had finished, Grace was obviously excited.

'That's brilliant', she said. 'You should write a column about it, Maggie.'

Grace was also a journalist, but she worked at *The City*'s rival newspaper and was a leading investigative reporter. We were the top two students in our journalism degree; however, she had managed to beat me by 2 per cent in our final paper giving her fame and glory, well at least it seemed that way at the time. Her top marks led her to being headhunted by the leading political paper. I avoided work and took off travelling around Asia and Europe for two years, working odd jobs before returning home and struggling for months to land any kind of media job. Years later we were still competitive, but we conducted ourselves in a ladylike manner and thus kept our friendship intact.

'You must be earning a bit at the paper by now I would have thought', she said. 'How long have you been there, five years?'

There were nods of agreement around the table, making me more even more embarrassed as this awkward conversation clearly had the attention of most people.

'Look, everyone, I really don't want to talk about this anymore', I said bluntly.

At that moment Tim butted in. 'While we're on the subject of cash, I know I should have dealt with this before I arrived tonight, but I completely misjudged my bank balance and I'm a little short after paying rent last week. I meant to ask you or Fran to help me out earlier today', he said, looking at me pleadingly.

Before the last syllable was out of his mouth the guilt I was harbouring from not paying the rent overwhelmed me and I had offered to pay for his dinner, saying it had been too long since I had shouted him. So much for the Saturn Return.

'You're a legend, Maggie. I'll cook for you next week to make it up to you', Tim said.

As I walked to the toilet a few minutes later I realised that if I didn't pay the rent that week the stress and anxiety of lying to my friends would send me mad. I had $600 in my savings account left from when I had been paid the week before, I needed to pay the rent ASAP and dinner was now going to cost me double the amount I had banked on. And if I didn't watch myself I would be offering to pay Tim's rent, too. It was Friday night and I wouldn't be able to afford to scratch myself until I got paid again the following Wednesday if I was going to have enough money in my account to pay rent.

What the hell is wrong with me? I thought. I can't afford to pay for Tim's dinner. Why can't I just be a normal person for one bloody second and shut the hell up?

An hour later we were discussing where to go after dinner and Max asked if anyone wanted another bottle of wine before settling the bill.

'Definitely', the six of us said in unison.

By this stage we had all slipped into happy drunkenness and I was no longer worried about how much money I was spending. I just wanted to have a good time and Max was annoying me. The party was heaving around us and most people had swapped tables to catch up with friends. I decided it was a good time to go see Eliza and give her the handbag.

Eliza was sitting at a table with her new boyfriend, Tom, and a whole lot of lawyers she used to work with. I looked around for a chair hoping I could sit down with her for five minutes and get away from the madness at my own table, but I was forced to stand.

'Are you having a good time?' she asked, after giving the handbag its due credit.

'It's a great party, I'm feeling a little drunk and Max is giving me a hard time, so nothing out of the ordinary', I joked. 'More importantly, though, are you having fun?' I asked.

'It's a wonderful night; I'm really happy. Your table looks like it's having a lively conversation. What's on the agenda, Max and Jem's decision to make us all fly to Malaysia to watch them wed?'

Max and Jem had never been anywhere in Asia, but had recently decided it would be a great idea to marry on a remote Malaysian island. I told Eliza I'd never thought they would go through with it and confided that I was terrified now it was official, as I had no idea how I was going to afford a plane ticket, let alone accommodation. Eliza said I'd have to get my act together quickly because I was a witness and had to be there.

Eliza had the sensitivity of a doormat, I thought. There were times when I was sure she was planted on earth to pull me up on the mistakes I had made or was about to. Either way, her comments about getting my act together made me happy there wasn't a chair free on her table and I headed back to sit with the others.

The night wore on and after ordering another two bottles of red, we got the bill. It was $150 each and I had to spot Tim. I was horrified. I knew it was a great restaurant, but it wasn't like it had a Michelin star. I paid our share and pretended it was water off a duck's back. I was also too drunk to realise the extent of the damage not paying rent would have on the equilibrium of my happy home.

The following week I found myself back outside Jack O'Brien's apartment building staring at the front doors. It had been close to three weeks since the rent was due and I still hadn't paid it. As much as I wanted to rid myself of the burden, Eliza's dinner had broken the bank and unless I waited another week I would have no money to buy even a loaf of bread. It would only be another nine days, I told myself. The real estate agent didn't seem to be fussed—well, he hadn't called.

I was sick of looking over my bank statements so I started to delve into O'Brien's sordid past to prepare myself on the off-chance I actually had an opportunity to speak to him. I had followed the trial sporadically, but didn't think I had enough knowledge to jump on him and start asking intelligent questions if he ever left his house—something I wasn't sure was ever going to happen.

O'Brien's business and family life was available at the click of a Google search and, surprisingly, what was known of his family seemed fairly normal. The youngest of two children—he had a sister—O'Brien was brought into the world by two Irish immigrant parents who travelled halfway around the world to start a new life away from poverty.

His father, Jack senior, started a construction company with his brother. The company went on to become very successful, which meant Jack junior was able to attend St Aloysius. St Al's, as it was known, was a posh private boys' school, which had produced two of our country's leaders and legions of well-known lawyers, bankers and doctors. Jack was head of the school in his final year and topped the class. He went on to study economics and law at university before heading to London to complete an MBA at the London School of Economics.

His dodgy dealings seemed to have started some time after he accepted a job as the chief financial officer at the corporate banking giant Shamrock Enterprises. The company had no connection with the luck of the Irish. It was a massive merchant bank owned by a Saudi Arabian family by the name of Shareef, who apparently once owned a beloved black stallion called Shamrock.

Shamrock Enterprises was as clean as a whistle, but, it was later revealed, the person the family chose to take the helm of the company was not so squeaky. Although the Shareefs never exposed why they decided to part ways with O'Brien, they made it very clear they wanted nothing to do with him ever again. When he left Shamrock, O'Brien went out alone and started what became the second-biggest Ponzi scheme in history.

By midday there was still no sign of O'Brien. His doorman was starting to stare at me sitting alone in the car and I had no doubt he knew what I was there for. Generally, on a stake-out of someone as newsworthy as Jack O'Brien there would have been several other news outlets champing at the bit to get him to talk. What was odd about this one, and I had done many, was there was no-one else around. My boss, Janice, had sent me to the job without a photographer, so even if I did manage to get a glimpse of the elusive man I wouldn't have been able to capture it on film—a seemingly critical component considering my chances of getting an exclusive interview were so slim.

Even though I wasn't supposed to leave my post, I had forgotten to make my lunch and I saw no reason a quick trip down the road for some food and a bathroom stop was out of order. O'Brien lived in the flashest part of the city, so there were some great places to grab food. Unfortunately, they were also some of the most expensive, and I ended up paying $20 for a salad sandwich and a takeaway coffee, something I had got into the habit of doing since I had started the stake-out.

As I walked back to my car I did a quick mental calculation of the money I had spent while sitting outside O'Brien's home. If I was correct, I had spent $400 in a month just on sandwiches and coffee. That couldn't be right, I thought. How could I have justified spending hundreds of dollars on lunches at work? I redid the calculation on my phone and the same figure came up. Damn it. I then decided to try to add up what I had spent on toast at the cafe at the base of *The City*'s building. I calculated I bought toast and coffee for $10 a pop about four times a week, not bad for someone with a wheat allergy.

I had been working at *The City* for five years and had purchased a $10 lunch most days without giving it a second thought. If I coupled the lunch with the breakfasts, excluding my five weeks annual leave, I was spending about $3120 on takeaway meals a year—a pretty hefty sum when I was earning only $53 500 a year. I also went out for dumplings every Thursday night with Max and Jem, which came to $30 each, including wine—providing we stuck to just one bottle. That was another $1560 right off the bat. No wonder I didn't have any bloody money.

My sums were depressing. I could have made myself a sandwich at home for a quarter of the price I had been paying. I vowed to eat breakfast at home and make my lunch from that day on. I mean, what was wrong with a bowl of cereal?

At 5.30 pm I arrived back at the newsroom and walked straight up to Janice to ask who was taking over from me at O'Brien's place.

'No-one', Janice said.

Janice had recently been made news chief after returning from a three-year post as the company's China correspondent. She was 32, divorced and, from what I could tell, perpetually unhappy. Although only a couple of years older then me, Janice had so far had a stellar career and while in China had broken two of the biggest stories to come out behind the red curtain in at least a decade. I respected her work, but personally I thought she was a bitch.

She was really starting to piss me off. If it was such an important story that they had to have me sitting outside O'Brien's place day in, day out, I couldn't figure out why the hell they weren't sending someone to watch him around the clock, but I didn't have the guts to confront her. The newsroom was buzzing as reporters finished their stories and the subeditors started laying out the pages of the next day's paper. I said hello to Genevieve, a Scottish immigrant who had become a close friend when we were placed next to one another in the office the year before.

'Any sign of O'Brien?' she asked sympathetically.

'Not a peep', I replied, sighing melodramatically. 'It's been weeks and Janice will not let me leave the outside of his penthouse. I'm starting to think she just hates me and wants me out of the office.'

'Don't be silly', Genevieve consoled. 'You are a wasted talent sitting out on your own, but just think about how good you'll feel when you get the scoop.'

Despite Genevieve's kind words, I went home demoralised that again I wouldn't have a story in the following day's paper and I would most likely be sent back out to O'Brien's. I had not had a byline for nearly a month and I was starting to get a bad case of journalist's paranoia — a strange phenomenon that occurs when reporters haven't had a story in the paper for weeks and they can almost see the grim reaper (the editor) banging down their door. Stake-outs were notoriously tough because you had to be on your guard in the off-chance the person you were trying to talk to actually appeared and more often than not it was the only job you were working on for the paper that day.

Tim was good to his word, and on the Friday night after Eliza's dinner I arrived home to find him cooking up a storm in the kitchen. Tim didn't make dinner enough for Fran and me considering his passion and penchant for cooking. Just the thought of eating some tasty food made me forget about work and I sat down at the kitchen counter to unwind from the crappy week at work with a glass of wine and opened three ominous letters with my name on them — credit card bills.

Everybody with a credit card has a love–hate affair with the cute little piece of plastic. My two cards were full to the brim. I had paid off the Universal card three times, but never closed the account, while the LAND card had only been activated on 10 December and was already maxed out. As far as I could see most of the purchases were made in the week leading up to Christmas. As well as the presents, there was also nearly $300 taken out in cash advances. And each time I withdrew money from my credit cards at an ATM I was slugged with a $5 cash advance fee. Why had I not noticed this before?

It was now more than two weeks into the new year, I had been paid twice and still hadn't paid rent and, apart from Eliza's birthday, this was the first meal I had eaten with either of my housemates in almost a month. I had avoided seeing them because I felt guilty and had spent most nights out and about. Fran had been at her new marketing job at the fashion house for a couple of weeks and I hadn't even had a chance to ask her how it was going.

We sat down to a perfectly grilled steak and polished off a bottle of red over the meal. Fran said her new job was going well and I told them that the O'Brien stake-out was starting to make me think I wasn't wanted at work. The three of us were single and 29. If we weren't living together I don't know what would have happened to us. Well, we probably wouldn't have drunk so much, but that was beside the point.

It was 29 January and I still hadn't paid the rent even though the money had been sitting in my account for two days. What kind of an idiot does that? When I got home that night I found Tim and Fran sitting at the kitchen table in the middle of what appeared to be a serious conversation. I put down my bag, grabbed my mail, slipped off my shoes and walked over to join them.

'The real estate agent called', Fran said gruffly.

My heart started thumping. I could feel the colour draining from my face and I immediately felt nauseated. My breathing quickened and I could feel pain streaking across my chest; I was having an anxiety attack.

'Oh, I think I know what that phone call might have been about', I said.

'He took a month off after Christmas and none of his colleagues had checked whether his tenants had paid their rent', Fran continued. 'Apparently we're short $1000 on this month's rent. And since Tim and I have both paid we're assuming you forgot to transfer your cash to the agent?'

I couldn't lie to their faces.

'I didn't exactly forget...' I began, and then blurted out the whole saga detail by detail. After I'd confessed I sat there for what seemed like hours. I didn't know what to say, I'd let down my friends. More than anything, though, I had been acutely embarrassed they would find out I didn't pay the rent, not because I couldn't afford it, but because I wanted to go to Eliza's birthday.

As though he could read my thoughts, Tim finally broke the silence and demanded to know why I had offered to pay for his share at Eliza's dinner when I had not paid the rent.

'I don't understand, Maggie', he said. 'I made an honest mistake when I forgot I had no cash the other night. There's no way I would have gone to Eliza's unless you or Fran had been able to spot me.'

Fran had not said a word for close to 10 minutes and my guilt was irrationally turning to anger.

'Okay you two, what's the big deal? Yes, I didn't pay, but the money will be in the landlord's account this week', I said.

'The agent said if the money is not paid by Monday, he will start the eviction process', Fran said.

'What?' I gasped. This was an agent who hadn't even been in contact to reprimand us earlier and now he was suddenly threatening eviction?

'He said the landlord is angry because he relies on our rent to pay the mortgage on his family home', Fran continued.

Things went even further downhill from there. Fran and Tim said they were bitterly disappointed in me and questioned whether there were other things I had put off paying.

'You know full well I have always been responsible when it comes to paying bills', I shouted. 'They might be late sometimes, but I'm not solely guilty of that crime. I don't know when the pair of you became so high and mighty. I said it was a mistake and do you honestly think I would have kept putting it off if I thought there was a chance we would all be chucked out?'

When I finished defending myself, Fran dropped another bombshell.

'The agent also said our rent is being raised another $100 a week. Tim and I are able to pay, but we don't think you'll be able to afford it, judging by the fact that you've just been scraping enough money together to pay thus far.'

I could not believe this was my friend Fran talking. She said they were not trying to be horrible, but I had been sneaking around behind their backs for weeks and they could see I had been stressed out of my mind about work and money for double that time.

'Maggie, this is our home. You can't not pay the rent and not think there are going to be serious repercussions. That's fine when you're 20 and living a transient lifestyle, but this is our life', Fran said. 'Neither Tim nor I have anyone else to fall back on. If we get evicted we lose our home and our bond. I've just given up a very well-paid job—as if I wasn't going to be angry!'

That was the moment my life went down the toilet. I was irrational and angry and on the defensive. I was so embarrassed that they were implying that I could go scrounge off my parents if I needed to. I could, but that was beside the point! I accused Tim and Fran of a number of terrible things, and I brought up secrets they had each told me in confidence and a huge fight ensued. I eventually went to my room and burst into tears.

I had no idea what I was going to do. This could not be happening to me. The last thing Fran had said to me had really hit home. I started to wonder if I took things like a having a beautiful home and the responsibilities of paying rent for granted. One thing I was sure of, there was no way my salary was going to be able to stretch to pay more rent on any house, no matter how much I wanted it to.

After what seemed like hours I slunk out of the house, jumped in the car and headed to Eliza's place to debrief. When I arrived she could see that I had been crying and ushered me into her kitchen for a cup of tea. I told her everything that had happened and she made me explain why I had not paid the rent to begin with.

'I can see where they're coming from, sweets', Eliza said in the most sympathetic tone she could muster.

'I know', I replied. 'I've acted like a total idiot. But I genuinely don't know what to do. Everything kind of got away from me after Christmas. I was working so hard and partying so much I think I had a momentary brain freeze and forgot my responsibilities.'

Eliza asked me what I was going to do next and I said I had absolutely no idea.

'What about staying at your parents' place for a while?' she suggested.

Mum and Dad's house was not an option. They had mentioned being worried about my lifestyle at Christmas and this would have just given them more ammunition.

'I'll pay this month's rent tomorrow. Then I have to pay next month's next week. That's another $1000 I don't have right at this moment. At least if I pay for February, Tim and Fran will have a month to find another housemate before the rent goes up.'

My theory sounded good on paper, but in reality it meant I would have no money for food or other bills. I had not paid a credit card bill for over a month and I had some unpaid parking fines to deal with—about $400 worth.

The realisation that I was going to have to move out of my beloved house so abruptly also brought on another problem—the bond. Fran had paid my bond when we moved in because she had found the house before Tim and I were even aware we were looking to move in together. I'd been living in a house with two couples, but I had been spending most nights in bed with Guy, my boyfriend at the time. Fran said she had seen the house and knew it was the perfect home for us and didn't hesitate to offer to pay the bond for me in return for moving in. How could I resist?

There was no way I was going to be able to scrape together enough money to move into another house. And there was no way I was going to confess this to anyone. After about the 10th cup of tea, Eliza offered me her spare room for the night. She had recently bought her first home. If I was irresponsible with my spendings, my dear friend was the complete opposite. A few months earlier she had started her own business as a barrister, after working as a high-flying solicitor in a city law firm for seven years. She obviously earned a hell of a lot more then me, but she had a whole lot more sense than I had cents.

The next morning I woke up at 6 and went home to get my gym and work gear before the other two were awake. The 30-minute swim did me the world of good. I arrived at the office just after 8.30 am and transferred the rent money straightaway. It was Friday morning and another day in the car looking at Jack O'Brien's doors did not faze me, as it was the end of the week. But Janice surprised me, sending me to cover the latest protest at a water desalination plant about two hours from the office. I was finally going to have a story in the paper—whoo hoo!

When I arrived home from work that evening I was surprised to see Eliza's car out the front of our house. I was prepared to go into damage control mode and sincerely apologise to Tim and Fran for my nasty outburst the night before, but Eliza's presence was going to make that awkward.

I had a massive dose of déjà vu when I walked in the door; Tim and Fran were seated at the table again, but this time Eliza was with them. They all cheerily greeted me and I started to feel freaked out.

'How was your day, sweets?' Eliza asked.

'Fine. What's going on here?' I replied nervously.

Fran explained that Eliza had called her that morning to say how upset I was. They started to chat about my options and thought they had a solution I would be happy with.

'I'm offering you my spare room, for $500 a month, effective immediately', Eliza said excitedly.

'That's very generous, Eliza, but I can't accept', I replied. 'You've just moved in and haven't stopped going on about how much you love living on your own.'

'Look,' she said, 'you'd actually be doing me a favour. It would take about 15 years off my mortgage repayments if you could contribute for a year. It would also take a hell of a lot of pressure off you to find a new place at short notice.'

The whole concept of having a mortgage and the time it takes to pay one off was completely foreign to me, but I didn't question that Eliza wouldn't have got her sums right. Fran and Tim had still not said a word to me, apart from hello.

'What about you two?' I said. 'How are you going to find someone to move in so quickly?'

'Already sorted', Tim said. 'Yvette's sister moved here from Paris last month and has agreed to take your room.'

'How convenient', I snapped, feeling suddenly even more betrayed. 'What were you going to do if I said no to Eliza's offer?'

'We knew you wouldn't', they annoyingly chimed.

I was in shock. On the one hand Eliza had offered me a lifeline, but the other two had been extremely quick to offload me.

'You really need to sort out your finances, Maggie', Fran said.

'I think I can safely say now that is absolutely none of your business', I spat back.

I agreed to move out the next day.

Lessons learned

- Don't ignore money issues – putting them off won't make them go away.

- Think before you buy – dinner, drinks, gifts, anything.

- Work out where you stand – what is your income? What are your expenses?

- Lying to your friends about money makes things worse.

- Always pay your rent on time!

PART II

Bad habits die hard

1 February to 22 April

Universal credit card: $5500 owing
LAND credit card: $1000 owing
Parking fines: $400
Happiness: non-existent

The evening following my 'eviction' on behalf of two of my closest friends, a lot of soul-searching went on. I was completely exposed. Everyone knew my darkest secret: I was terrible with money. But now that it was out in the open I was determined to get my act together. Although initially shocked that Tim and Fran had acted so swiftly and dramatically, in retrospect it was the nicest thing they could have done as they'd saved me $500 rent that I couldn't afford. And, as I looked back over the last few months, I realised things had been going downhill for a while.

When the three of us had moved in together 18 months earlier I was so eager to show off to my new housemates that I contributed several small, but very expensive, pieces of furniture for our shared living spaces, our kitchen had the latest state-of-the-art gadgets and the fridge was always stocked with lovely food I just happened to pick up from the amazing organic deli and market on my way home from the office. All this on my $53 500 a year salary.

Other acts of economic food-foolery included buying groceries I would never eat. Most weekends I would have no problem walking to our local cafe and spending at least $20 on poached eggs, toast and coffee when there was already fresh free-range eggs and bread in my kitchen at home. And I would stock up on food for midweek meals, but was never at home to cook and it eventually all went in the bin after the rank smell wafting from the fridge convinced me I was not going to cook the salmon, bok choy and broccoli stir-fry with fresh lemongrass recommended in *The City* food section the week before.

My extravagances did not stop in the home. On top of eating out several nights a week and buying my breakfast and lunch most days, I also wore nice clothes, had my hair blow-dried once a week, had a gym membership I rarely used and always had the latest iPod, iPhone, Apple laptop and speakers so everything was white and in sync, just as Steve God, I mean Jobs, had intended. It was common practice for me to spend at least $300 per week on taxis, dinner and drinks, and I would often offer to pay for others, even though I knew I could not afford it. Sometimes I would walk into my favourite clothing store just to have a look at the new season range and find I had walked out with more than $500 worth of clothes, just because I had to have them. I wouldn't say this kind of thing happened all the time, but it happened enough for me to be broke most Mondays before payday.

As far as I could tell, there was absolutely no reason for my bad relationship with money. As a child and teenager I wanted for nothing, and my relationship with my parents was as strong a bond a child could have with two adults—apart from when they were giving me a hard time. My mother, Joan, was a banking executive who had endlessly tried to instil a firm grasp of the benefits of financial independence in her only daughter's life. Every Christmas from the age of 18 she had given me the latest self-help book on money or the latest investing bible from Warren Buffett, which had absolutely no effect on my ability to handle my finances—and I had absolutely no grasp of investing. I came from a long line of women who thought it was essential for a woman to have total control of every aspect of their lives—this meant their money, their men and their children. I must have had some kind of bizarre genetic deficiency to miss out on such a strong familial trait.

When I called Max to ask him to help me move, he was wary.

'Why are you moving out? Or shouldn't I ask?' he said.

I had decided to be honest and tell him everything. I didn't leave out a single gory detail, even telling him how I had conspired to keep putting off paying the rent until the real estate agent called me for an explanation. As soon as I had finished, I got embarrassed. Max's reaction didn't help.

'How old are you? Didn't you listen to a word I said about the Saturn Return? This is your big chance to change things', was all he said before I started to defend myself.

'I think we both know I feel like a complete loser right now, so don't make things worse than they already are by bringing up silly superstitions. Can you please help me move? They want me out today', I said.

Max said he would be over at about 4 pm, which gave me enough time to go to the supermarket and grab some old boxes to pack up my things. On returning I walked into the kitchen and Fran was washing her breakfast dishes. I hadn't planned to apologise so quickly, but after several hours of brewing about my actions there wasn't much left for me to do.

'I'm sorry for being so rude to you last night. When you said I didn't respect this house as your home I felt like a complete idiot. I behaved horrendously and I understand if you want me out of your life', I said to her.

'Maggie, I don't think you're a bad person. Tim and I both love you. The phone call from the real estate agent just gave us a huge fright. I know I used to earn a lot more money than you, but I've just quit my job and am now on three-quarters of my old salary. I can only afford to live here because of the money I saved while working for the government. And Tim is putting away everything he earns so he can start his own business.'

'I do know all that, and I'm sorry. Anyway, I just wanted to let you know I'm moving out today. Max is coming to help me this afternoon. I can leave most of this kitchen stuff here for you guys to use as Eliza's place is decked out already.'

Always the sweetheart, Fran said there was still a week before the new housemate moved in and asked me round for one more dinner with her and Tim. I told her I wanted to settle in, but promised to see them both soon.

Eliza lived in a single-storey terrace about 10 kilometres from the house I was leaving, on the north side of the city and approximately five kilometres from work. I had stayed at her place a number of times since she had moved in, but I hadn't payed any attention to the room I would now call my own. When I arrived with Max, my clothes, computer, chair, bookshelf and books, Eliza opened the door and I could immediately see into my new bedroom. There was a large window facing the wide leafy street, a queen-size bed and a newly painted built-in wardrobe. She had painted the room white and hung thick, gold, floor-to-ceiling curtains on the window and a huge mirror rested above the out-of-use fireplace. My new room was bigger than the one I had left behind.

Eliza helped Max and me get my stuff into the house, then left me to settle in. It was a lovely room, but it didn't feel like home. Just after 6 pm, I was lying on my new bed, feeling sorry for myself, when Eliza knocked on the door and asked me to come to the kitchen. She told me to sit down and pushed a glass of wine in front of me.

'Okay. I don't mean to be harsh, but we really have to set some ground rules. I'm more than happy for you to stay here as long as you want. However, the main objective of letting you stay with me for a fraction of the amount of rent I should be charging you is to help you get your money in order. I don't want you to think I don't want you here, but you know how much I've been looking forward to living on my own, so this is a sacrifice. As you are my best friend, and I know you don't want to ask anyone for help, I have offered you my home so you can sort your shit out.'

It was the second time in two days one of my closest friends had felt the need to have a go at me—I just didn't understand it! I had only put off paying my rent. You'd have thought I was a drug addict needing some kind of an intervention.

'You have no idea how grateful I am. This has happened so quickly. I just need a day to figure a few things out', I told her, hoping she would get the idea that I didn't want to talk about it with her.

Before I could say anything else, she was off again in her most matter-of-fact barrister manner.

'That's all good and well, sweets. What I really need to see is action. I'm going to help you get your life sorted. Tell me, how do you plan to change things?'

I'd been thinking about nothing but money for weeks and still hadn't managed to save a cent or make even a small dent in my debts. I told her the fact I was going to be saving $500 a month on rent was going to be the biggest help I could have been given.

'But what are you going to do about the rest of your problems? The rent did not get you into the situation you were in', she said.

Eliza was a whiz at handling her cash. She had successfully put herself through university, bought her own home and had still had the tens of thousands of dollars needed to set up her own legal chambers — quite a formidable task for any 30 year old. She was also one of the kindest people I had ever met, even if she was a ball-breaker. Although I had never said a word to her about my bank balances, it did not surprise me that she had turned up at my house the night before to be my knight in shining armour.

'I'm not going to be looking over your shoulder, but you have to understand I'm doing you a huge favour here. If you don't want to move in indefinitely, you're more than welcome to stay for a month until you get some bond money together and find a new share house.'

Just hearing the word 'share' made me shudder. There was no way I could go back to sharing a bathroom with strangers. I was almost 30 for heaven's sake.

'Do you want me to show you a budget or something?' I asked, hoping that she would say no. I also decided to keep my mouth shut about the list I had made on New Year's Day for fear she would ask to see that too.

'Not at all. I just want you to think about the things you can change', she replied.

After Eliza had laid down the law, she got some cheese from the fridge, a bottle of red wine and a sneakily hidden packet of cigarettes, and we drank and smoked while I did all I could to keep the conversation on everything else going on in our lives that didn't involve money.

Eliza had started going out with a man called Tom not long after she bought the house. Tom was a 40-year-old geologist from South Africa who was in the country to study some kind of fossil neither of us had ever heard of. They had met though a friend she had done her legal clerkship with and she was obviously falling in love, or she suddenly knew a lot about granite. Either way, she was in a good place.

There was not much love to talk about on my front. I had broken up with a guy called Guy in September and had absolutely no intention of getting into a relationship for the foreseeable future. Guy was great on paper, crap in reality. We met at a conference I was covering for the paper on health care. His family owned 20 private nursing homes that catered for the needs of the rich elderly. He doggedly pursued me, which was highly flattering. When I finally gave in and fell for him he started a torturous cat-and-mouse game where he would break up with me one week, break my heart, and then come crawling back a week later. About a year after we first met, I decided I had had enough and dumped him. I was acting like all the dimwitted females I had relentlessly criticised throughout my 20s and getting him out of my life was the most liberating thing I had done in years. This was not to say I was immune to a charming man's advances. He just had to have the right intentions.

After talking until midnight, Eliza and I fell into our beds about a quarter of the way through the second bottle of wine. I slept like a baby for the first night in weeks and when I finally dragged myself out of bed the next morning I grabbed the Sunday papers, my laptop and walked around the corner to my new local cafe, a little place with great coffee and a view of the park. I was on a mission to be in control. The latest credit card bills were in my bag. I had also brought along every receipt for every purchase I'd made in the previous six months — only because I never cleaned out my wallet. I ordered a coffee and pulled out the first statement.

My Universal credit card statement said I owed $5500 and I was $35 overdrawn. I couldn't figure out why I had overspent on the card as I'd kept track of every purchase up to the last $15 I had spent on petrol on 30 December — the last time I'd used the card before it was declined. I had seen my mother pouring over her and my father's statements when she was doing their taxes, so I got out a highlighter and scanned the bill. As far as I could see the calculations I had made were right. I seemed to be over the limit because of late payment fees.

My second statement was for my LAND credit card. In late November I had been dawdling online at work and on a whim decided to apply for the LAND bank's latest low-interest credit card with a $1000 limit to get me through Christmas. I justified applying for it because my Universal card was getting close to being maxed out. I thought if I had another card I could just pay off the Universal card on a monthly basis rather than constantly using and worrying about it. I was more than a little surprised when my application for the LAND card was accepted and I received the card in the post a week later.

My amateur strategy hadn't worked. The LAND card had been activated on 10 December and it had taken me less than two weeks to max it out, with all of the transactions occurring in the week leading up to Christmas. My intention had been to use the card to pay off $400 in parking fines I had accumulated and pay for a couple of Christmas presents. I'd told myself I would then pay off the balance in full. I could see from the statement I had held off using the card for another 10 days before the carnage began.

LAND Low-Interest Credit Card				
Overdue	**Opening balance**	**New charges**	**Payments**	**Closing balance**
$0.00	$0.00	$995.00	$0.00	$995.00

Date	Transaction details	Amount (A$)
20 Dec	Tivoli Audio	$350.00
20 Dec	The City Subscriber Service	$180.00
20 Dec	LAND ATM, CBD	$120.00
20 Dec	Cash advance withdrawal fee	$5.00
21 Dec	Babylon Restaurant Pty Ltd	$80.00
21 Dec	LAND ATM, Richmond	$50.00
21 Dec	Cash advance withdrawal fee	$5.00
23 Dec	General Hotel, Fitzroy	$100.00
23 Dec	LAND ATM, Richmond	$100.00
23 Dec	Cash advance withdrawal fee	$5.00

Credit limit $1000   Available credit $5.00

My intentions had started well, but were not sustained. I had bought my parents a Tivoli radio and a yearly subscription to *The City* for Christmas. I was then supposed to pay off the parking fines and clear the credit ledger with my next pay. I didn't need the statement to know that hadn't happened. I had blown $450 on partying in the lead-up to Christmas, leaving me with zero credit. Again, not surprisingly, I was left with no money.

I needed to pay off both credit cards ASAP. I decided the best way to get ahead would be to set up a transfer from my savings account before I had a chance to access it. The Universal card was the oldest and, judging from the latest statement, it had the highest interest rate so it had to go first. I logged on to my internet banking and was dismayed to see I only had $170 in my savings account to last me until the Wednesday after I had paid my rent on my old place. I set up a weekly transfer of $150 to the Universal card with the intention of cutting up the card as soon as I got home. That would mean the card would be cleared and closed by the end of September. I would just pay the minimum on the LAND card until I had cleared the Universal card.

I was on a roll, so I decided to write a list of my regular bills that I could put money aside for from each pay. I earned $772 a week post-tax and about $3400 a month.

Monthly expenses:

- $500 rent to Eliza
- $500 (approx.) on my credit cards
- $300 on bills
- $800 on food and drinks
- $700 on miscellaneous spending

Total monthly expenses = about $2800.

The rest of the money, about $600, could be saved. It all seemed so simple; I was easily going to be able to get myself out of debt. I wasn't sure why I hadn't done a budget before. I could probably afford to put a couple of hundred more on the cards as well, I thought proudly.

I felt fantastic. It wasn't even 11 am on a Sunday and I had figured out a way to pay off my credit card without ever having to think about it again and, for the first time in months, I could see where my money was going. I had even refrained from the greasy breakfast I was craving.

February was going to be all about saving. Eliza's place was about five kilometres from work and I decided to cancel my gym membership and walk to work every day, saving myself another $60 per month and getting me the exercise that I so desperately needed. Lunches were no longer going to be bought on the run. On the way home from the cafe I stopped at my new supermarket and stocked up on bread, eggs, cereal, instant coffee, salad and a bottle of wine for good measure for the week ahead, leaving me with $100 in my savings account till Tuesday.

When I got home Eliza and Tom were splayed out on the living-room floor playing Scrabble and watching a movie. I didn't know Tom that well but I was so proud of myself I didn't feel any shame in telling them both about my productive morning.

'What about transport, petrol, parking, going out, clothes and the like?' Eliza asked as soon as she had seen my single-column budget.

'I'm going to be walking to work, so the car, petrol and parking are no problem. I have no intention of going shopping for at least two months and I have factored my social life into my budget', I said.

'I'll leave you to it then I guess', she said.

I was dejected. I had tried to make a fresh start and less than 24 hours after moving into her home Eliza had already lectured me twice. Who was this person I had moved in with, my mother? Eliza said she would not be looking over my shoulder, but it was only day two and she was already annoying the hell out of me. When Tom stepped out to buy us all dinner I asked her when she had become so bossy.

'After I quit my job at the law firm, bought a house and spent more than $30000 setting up my own legal practice', she replied. 'I know what it takes to get things happening. You may not realise it, Maggie, but you have been worrying about money for years. You are either overzealous, over generous or completely broke. I know you've worked hard to get where you are at the paper, and it doesn't pay a whole lot, but there are plenty of people who earn a hell of a lot less than you who are in far better positions financially.'

I believed her. I had recurring thoughts that if I was debt free and had money in the bank, I would be a happier, kinder and more fulfilled human being. Just as if I had lost the five kilograms a year ago that had suddenly turned into 10 kilograms. I really wanted to sort my money problems out once and for all. The problem was I had absolutely no faith in my ability to do it. Some people just aren't programmed to be good with money.

Monday morning, 2 February, I got up and reluctantly ate a bowl of cereal and ran out the door for work. I was never going to make it to the office on time on foot—it would have taken me about an hour to walk—so I jumped in the car and vowed to get up 30 minutes earlier the next day so I would have ample time. It wasn't a big deal anyway. The car park only cost $11 a day if you arrived before 9.30 am, which wasn't that much, and the train would have cost me $7.50. So realistically, there wasn't a great deal of difference. Besides, I had already saved myself $10 by eating cereal at home.

After the weekend from hell I was ecstatic when Janice told me I would have the pleasure of working from the office and get to act like a reporter, as well as catch up with my colleagues. I was given the task of going to the airport to report on Jay Wilson, a superstar country and western singer who was arriving in Australia late morning. He had a massive fan base and a legion of them was expected to be waiting for his arrival. I was not going to meet him, I was told to go and get among the masses; it was going to be hilarious.

'Where have you been Maggie?' the paper's senior crime writer, Dave, said to me as I walked through the room to my desk.

Dave was a pompous 35 year old with a penchant for young female journalists and bad berets.

'I've been tailing O'Brien', I said far more confidently than I felt.

'On Sunday Island?' he asked smugly.

'No, at his apartment', I said, rolling my eyes at Dave's unwelcome questioning.

'Who sent you over there? It's a well-known fact Jack O'Brien has been holidaying with his wife and daughters on Sunday Island for the past three weeks. Haven't you been watching the news?' he said, smirking.

Dave was such an idiot and he had absolutely no shame. About six months earlier he had tried to crack on to me at a bar after work one night. He had sidled up next to me and while fondling his red beret, said he liked my work. I politely told him to nick off, but he had held it against me ever since. I wasn't alone though, he had tried it on with every girl in the office.

In this case, he had actually told me something I didn't know. No wonder there were no other journalists at O'Brien's place. Before he could say anything else to me I had spun around and marched over to Janice's desk.

'O'Brien's on holiday?' I said through clenched teeth.

'Yes, of course. Where did you think he was?'

I could feel my face getting redder by the second. 'Possibly at home seeing as that's where you've had me staked out?'

'I had you out there just in case he came back early. It seems he's enjoying the sun and I'm sending our new reporter, Spencer, to the island to keep an eye on him for the next week before he is due home.'

I couldn't believe what I was hearing. After all the work I had done, she was sending someone else on an island stake-out—that should have been my island stake-out.

'You don't think I could have handled the assign-ment?' I asked.

'I need you working on other things,' Janice said without even looking up at me.

To say I was upset was a gross understatement; I was psychotic with rage. I walked out of the building, called Genevieve's extension and asked her to meet me downstairs. I then walked across the road and bought the first packet of cigarettes I had purchased in more than six months. I opened the pack, took out a cigarette, lit it and inhaled. I instantly felt better and worse at the same time. I finished the first cigarette and was about to light the second when Genevieve walked around the corner.

'Who's Spencer?' I immediately asked.

'How are you too? And when did you start smoking again?' Genevieve replied.

'Sorry. I'm having a very shitty day.'

'No kidding. Spencer was poached from *The Observer*. You must have heard about him. He won the by-line award for helping expose O'Brien's Ponzi scheme two years ago. Why do you want to know about him anyway?'

'Because he's been sent to sunny Sunday Island to keep an eye on O'Brien at the tail end of the scumbag's month-long sojourn', I replied. 'Janice said I was at his place in case he came back early.'

'Okay, you were right. She really doesn't like you. Don't hold it against Spencer, though. He seems lovely and, if I might say so myself, the first attractive man to walk through *The City*'s doors in my short tenure as single woman at large.'

Before we returned upstairs we smoked another cigarette together and organised to have a drink that night with anyone else in the office who was up for it. I hoped all my good work planning to save and quitting smoking had not just backfired. I was like a moth to a flame when it came to stress, cigarettes and a good night out.

To add insult to injury, when I returned from meeting Jay Wilson's hysterical throng of fans—each and every one decked out in a Stetson and cowboy boots—my new assignment was to act as Spencer's assistant. He was out of contact on the island, but he had left a list of instructions for me before he had flown out the night before. He wanted me to try to track down O'Brien's estranged older sister, Margaret, who lived on a farm near the coast, about an hour from the city. He had left her last-known address and told me to head out to her place as soon as I could.

He said my motive for talking to her was to see if she was willing to speak about her brother on the record. I was to ask her about Jack's childhood, where she had thought his life had gone astray and whether she thought her brother was a criminal. Considering they were estranged it seemed highly unlikely that she was going to have anything nice to say about him, let alone want to speak to me and divulge family secrets. Spencer was obviously getting his directive from our editor, as she had said our goal was to find out as much information as possible to ruin O'Brien's reputation.

I drove out to the property and knocked on Margaret O'Brien's door. There was no answer and after my luck with her brother I wasn't keen to sit around and wait for someone to turn up. I figured I could just come back the next day. I decided to have a quick look around before I headed back to the office.

The farmhouse must have been at least a century old and had wisteria vines winding around every corner. About 500 metres from the house you could see ocean over a sheer cliff face. It was pretty spectacular. There were no cars in the open garage and as there were no neighbouring houses within eyesight I saw no harm in having a quick look in the mailbox to make sure I had the right address, but all the mail was addressed to a Mrs Black. As I was walking back to my car I noticed a woman in a broad-brimmed straw hat with netting hanging off it walking towards me.

'Mrs Black?' I asked sheepishly.

'Yes. Did you find what you were looking for in my mail?' she asked, taking the letters I was still holding.

'I'm so sorry. I'm Maggie Rose, a journalist from *The City*. I must have been given the wrong house. I was looking for a Margaret O'Brien.'

'No, you have the right place. I'm Margaret Black, nee O'Brien. I assume you're here to talk about my brother.'

I could feel my face burning with embarrassment, but Margaret Black was obviously not the least bit surprised to find a journalist on her doorstep, or front gate as it was. It was not a great way to try to get an interview.

She took off her hat to talk to me and I judged she must have been about 55 years of age, but she looked closer to 45 without the big hat on. She was tall, curvy, had perfect, fair (botoxed?) skin and short, black Isabella Rossellini hair. I wanted to be her instantly—or at least when I grew up.

From my experience knocking on random people's front doors, I knew it was best to just be upfront. I explained my reason for being there and said I would understand if she did not want to talk; however, I added there was a significant amount of public interest in her brother and we, *The City*, would not be the last newspaper to come and ask questions.

'You are, in fact, the first reporter to show up for an interview', Margaret said. 'I thought someone would have found me years ago, but it appears my second marriage went unnoticed. How did you find out I was here?'

'I was asked to come here by a colleague who had your address. I don't know why no-one else has turned up, I guess everyone thought they knew everything. Or didn't know about you at all. Would you be willing to have a quick chat with me?' I asked.

She said she'd give me 10 minutes because she had a prior engagement. That was all I needed, and I just kept thanking God I hadn't left without being a sticky beak. As we walked over to the house Margaret said she had been waiting for someone to show up and ask questions for a long time.

'I followed Jack's court case and prepared myself for an onslaught of journalists banging down my door. After the trial ended and he was released I think I was a little disappointed no-one ever came. There were things I needed to get off my chest. I know it's uncouth to air one's dirty laundry to the press, but Jack hurt a lot of people.'

Looking around the room it appeared that Margaret lived on her own. The only photos on the walls were dated and from what I could tell were of her and her parents.

She said up until she was 30, she and Jack were very close. She described him as the golden boy everybody wanted to be or be with. Margaret was five years older than her brother and said, initially, they only fell away from each other because she had started a family and he had moved overseas to continue his studies. As far as she could tell something went wrong when Jack started his MBA in London. He ceased all contact with his parents and only sporadically sent his sister letters and gifts for her growing family.

'Just before he went to work at Shamrock he came home and saw us all for two weeks and something had changed. He had recently married and didn't even bring his bride home to meet Mum and Dad, and he just criticised everything. Our parents had worked so hard to give us what their parents couldn't and here was their darling son treating them like scum. It was awful to watch and one of the last times Jack and I were ever in the same room together. Something had happened to him.'

His parents must have done something to him, was my first thought. No son would just turn on his parents like that.

'What had happened?' I asked.

'Without having said so much as a word about working for Shamrock in the two weeks he was home, suddenly on the last day he announced he had been offered the job as chief financial officer. And as I'm sure you know, the job catapulted him into the financial stratosphere', Margaret continued sadly.

'But I bet even Jack didn't think it would end as badly as it did.'

I was intrigued. What had happened to Jack O'Brien to make him such a slimeball? I knew there was a fall out with Shamrock Enterprises, but the tone of Margaret's voice made me think there was a whole lot more to it than anyone knew. Despite initially thinking she might have been a bit of a crackpot, after hearing her story I decided she was a normal person who was deeply disappointed in her younger brother. Before I got a chance to ask another question she said she had to go. I gave her my card and told her I would call within the week to talk more. I wouldn't say she looked glad to hear I would be back in touch, but I was — I had a lead on the story.

As I was driving back to the city I realised I had forgotten to make my lunch. So much for the first day of living thin. I was hopeless, how could I have forgotten to make a bloody sandwich? There wasn't much I could do about it, so I stopped at the first bakery I saw on the road and grabbed a roll and a coffee for the drive home.

When I got back to the office I tracked down a number for Spencer and was surprised when it rang and he answered.

'Hi, Spencer? This is Maggie Rose from the newsroom. I was just going to leave a message on your voicemail because I heard you were out of range.'

'Hi, Maggie. The reception is pretty dodgy, but if I walk to the ninth hole on the golf course I seem to get some action. Did you get my note?'

He had a gruff voice, which I quite liked. It almost made me forget that I should be mad to hear that he was on the golf course while I was schlepping around doing the hard work for him!

'Yeah, thanks. I found Margaret O'Brien and she was quite willing to talk. She hasn't spoken to her brother in years, but she said something about Shamrock that made me think she knows things no-one else does.'

He seemed genuinely impressed with my information and asked if I had reported my progress to Janice yet. I told him I hadn't quite got around to letting her know, because I didn't think I had anything we could use for the next day's paper.

'In my experience, it's best to say you didn't have any luck otherwise she might send you back out there', Spencer replied.

Who was this nice man on the other end of the phone with the gruff voice? I had been working at *The City* for five years and no-one had ever given me any advice. He was actually making me feel good about myself. I decided I wanted to meet this Spencer character.

'We need more from her to get a story up. She hasn't yet told you anything we didn't know. Has Janice told you we'll be working together for a while?'

'Not in so many words', I answered.

'I'm really sorry to drag you off your usual work, but I'm going to need some help on this story while I'm stuck on this island. I'm not getting anywhere because he knows I'm here and therefore is on his best behaviour.'

Spencer was apologetic as he gave me my next list of tasks. He said I was to head to the State Library and go through the microfiche newspaper archives and catalogue O'Brien's rise to stardom. This was something I was more than happy to do. I would be working out of the office, but not out of a car.

After work I went for what was supposed to be one drink with Genevieve because I had to drive home. True to form, one drink turned into five, and then we decided to grab a quick dinner before heading home. More wine was bought on the way and the cheap Chinatown meal turned into a $50-a-head affair. By the time I paid the $15 taxi fare home I was back to being broke. It wouldn't have been a Monday if I'd had cash leftover anyway, I thought. I was hopeless. My first day of saving and I had failed miserably. I needed to focus. I had to do it. I was sick of having no money.

The first four weeks of my savings plan were excruciating. By 28 February I had managed to walk to work only seven times, eat breakfast at home 10 times and make 15 lunches. I had budgeted $800 for food and drinks for the month and in the first fortnight I had done two $150 supermarket shops and probably thrown out $100 worth of food. There was one other problem: I secretly hated cereal. I was much more a piece of toast and a cup of tea kind of girl and trying to stomach a bowl of bran and wheat flakes with milk first thing in the morning turned my stomach. For some reason I had the ridiculous notion in my head that cereal was to be eaten if I was going to save money, but by the end of the month I realised I was just wasting cash on food that would never be eaten, so I stopped buying it.

Apart from the cereal I was still throwing out way more food than I was consuming and I was starting to feel incredibly guilty. This was not a matter of me not liking the food I was making; this was all about time. I was a naturally late person who did everything at the last minute. That's why I was a journalist; deadlines suited my personality. Well, that's what I told myself anyway.

Although I was struggling to sort out my breakfasts and lunches, dinners were going very well. I loved living with Eliza. Even though she was bossy as hell, we had a great time together and it didn't take me long to feel completely at home. We took turns cooking the evening meal and I was at home four nights a week rather than gallivanting around town — a miracle.

The nights I was hitting the town also meant a battle with the hairdryer. I had been going to the hairdresser once a week to have my long locks professionally blow-waved since I was 17 and whenever I had attempted to do it myself ended in tears. I had justified paying the $50 a week because it made me feel so good, but now I needed to save the cash and I was smart enough to know practise made perfect. I bought myself a good-quality round brush and hit the bathroom. The first few attempts were less than impressive. To begin with, my hair fell a third of the way down my back and I struggled to reach the ends, which meant only half my head was completed before I gave up and swept my hair into a ponytail. Then I rediscovered the hot rollers my parents had given me about 15 years earlier. I wouldn't say I looked like Gisele, but my hair looked a sight better than it had following my earlier efforts.

Eliza, with her naturally lovely curls, and Grace, who had a stylish short do, never understood how confident and sexy I would feel walking out of a salon and they would more often than not tell me I was wasting money. It was an addictive transformation and a quick trip to the hairdresser for a wash and dry could heal the scars of the worst week, which in my mind made it worth every cent.

On the work front I had been spending most of my mornings working out of the library recovering documents on O'Brien for Spencer and, as much as I liked being out of the office, Janice wanted me back each lunchtime where she would give me a pile of pictures to write captions for. It was a job a junior cadet should have been doing, not someone with five years up her sleeve. I wasn't hearing much from Spencer himself and I was getting worried all my hard work would go unnoticed on his return. Whenever that was.

My credit card payment plan seemed to be going well. I had paid $650 off my Universal card and another $50 had gone on the LAND card. But the $600 I said would go into saving each month hadn't eventuated and I had no idea where I had gone wrong. I looked through my statements and, as I had also started trying to limit how many times I was going to the ATM after watching a documentary on banks, I couldn't work out what I had been spending my money on.

On 10 March Spencer finally returned to the newsroom after finishing up with O'Brien and taking some leave. The day before I thought he was arriving back in the office he called me to make a time to go over in person what we had both come up with. I had been juggling my regular reporter duties following breaking news for the last week with going to the library and researching O'Brien.

After not hearing from him for a week after he had asked me to start researching, he had started calling me daily for updates, which became the highlight of my day—there was always a hint of flirting on both ends of the phone and I was dying to find out what he looked like.

Our first meeting would have been called professional suicide on my part. I had just hung up the phone after speaking to him, thinking he was still away, and was wondering whether his looks matched his interesting voice, so I sent an email to Genevieve demanding she tell me what he looked like. I could see her on the other side of the room, but she didn't look up and catch my eye like she normally would after I emailed her. Then I got a response.

From: Spencer Lee
Sent: Monday 10 March 11:57 AM
To: Maggie Rose
Subject: RE:

I have black hair, am wearing a navy suit and am sitting to your right behind Dave, so you can tell me if you think I'm hot.

Spencer

....

From: Maggie Rose
Sent: Monday 10 March 11:55 AM
To: Spencer Lee
Subject:

At least tell me if Spencer's hot or not!

Maggie

I was mortified. I had accidentally sent Spencer the email that was supposed to go to Genevieve. I was about to bolt across the newsroom to the bathroom and hide when I looked up to see an attractive 30-something, dark-haired man walking across the room towards me, smiling.

'I assume you're Maggie. Were you worried you wouldn't be able to find me at our meeting?' he asked, still smiling.

Being the idiot I was, I pretended I had no idea what he was talking about.

'You must be Spencer. I was talking about someone else, though. The email wasn't about you', I said, turning back to my computer and trying to pretend I had indeed sent him an email, but it was about someone else called Spencer who I wanted to know was hot.

'I'll see you later then. By they way, when do you want to meet up and go through our O'Brien investigation?' he said, still standing at my desk. He was making me feel weird. I could see his reflection in my computer screen and he was still smiling.

'Let me know when you're free', I said without turning around. I didn't want him to see my beetroot-red face.

As soon as he'd gone, I walked over to Genevieve, grabbed her by the scruff of the neck and demanded she come for lunch.

'It's been a while since I've seen anyone act like such a fool. Well done, Maggie. You're my hero', Genevieve said when I had told her about my emails going astray.

'Do you think he believed me?'

'Not a hope in hell.'

Genevieve and I may have only been friends for a short time, but she had already been privy to several embarrassing emails I had sent to the person I was writing about. I had forwarded them on to her to gauge the appropriate level of embarrassment I should have been feeling.

'You seem to have a problem separating your mind from your hands', she said, laughing.

'They need a muzzle', I said.

'I think you like Spencer', she said after we had ordered a sandwich.

'I don't even know him', I shot back a bit too quickly.

There was no denying it. Spencer was a bona fide handsome man. He had an incredibly commanding presence and seemed, from our daily conversations about O'Brien, like a genuinely good human being. I knew he was single and I had a big enough ego to think he thought I looked pretty good too from the way he was smiling when he walked across the room to greet me.

Oh dear. Yes, I had a crush.

Having a crush on someone was a welcome distraction from my money woes. I had forgotten how nice it was to get dressed up and flirt at work; Spencer didn't seem to pay much attention to me, though. We continued to work together and, despite my acute embarrassment about the email demanding to know what he looked like and a few stray glances, he ended up becoming more of a mentor than anything else. He seemed to have a lot of faith in my investigative abilities; a side of journalism I had not really focused on, as I had always wanted to be a columnist.

My dreams of having my own column were slowly dwindling as I was forced to write story after story about grandmothers' 100th birthdays and churn out regurgitated press releases. There wasn't much I could do about it, as Janice had me on a very short leash.

It was late April. I had knocked $1800 off my Universal credit card debt and I was starting to get into a groove making my lunch on a daily basis, despite my strange desire to want to spend money on food made fresh by someone else. Not using the card was a struggle to say the least. My hand would automatically reach in and grab it whenever I was short of cash. I had to train myself to say no. My combat method was to say a mantra to myself every day: '$5000 credit card debt, parking fines, no savings. $5000 credit card debt, parking fines, no savings'. If this wasn't going to make me feel bad, nothing was.

I continued to drive to work, which was costing me a lot more than I could realistically afford. The genetic defect that made me incapable of living thin, I decided, also made it physically and psychologically impossible for me get out of bed before 7.45 am. Most days, by the time I had showered and eaten, I had no choice but to drive. If I was really going to knock the debt on the head I had to stop using the car. It was costing me about $80 a week to run, including petrol and parking. I wasn't even going to get into the parking fine situation. I was just hoping to avoid a court marshal. There was one positive — I may have had fines, but I hadn't received a ticket for months, since the year before in fact.

Eliza always left for work an hour before me, so I honestly thought I had gotten away with driving to work. Little did I know she had a spy. Our neighbour was a 16-year-old girl called Charlotte who had a big crush on my best friend because she too wanted to work in law, so Eliza took the opportunity to use her to check on me. When Eliza confronted me about the driving I asked how she had found out and she admitted to asking Charlotte to watch me. Neither of us was going to win the argument; we both looked like idiots and a truce was called after I promised to start pounding the pavement again as soon as I could afford to buy new runners and Eliza said she would leave Charlotte alone. I was a terrible liar, but who the hell uses a 16 year old as their personal private detective?

Disaster struck one morning when my car stopped dead in its tracks on a major thoroughfare. No noises, no smoke, just dead. I called my car insurance company and as I hadn't renewed my membership I was going to have to pay the $150 rejoining fee over the phone. This required a credit card. For the first time since the New Year I was going to use my card. I was proud of myself. I paid the fee using my Universal card and waited for the roadside mechanic to turn up.

Then I received a frantic call from Janice on the news desk. 'Where are you?' she shouted down the phone.

'On my way to work. My car's broken down so I'm going to be late', I replied.

'We've just had a tip that O'Brien is heading out to the airport en route to London. You have to get to the airport now, Maggie. Leave your car where it is and get a taxi', she ordered.

As soon as Janice hung up, I frantically phoned all of my friends. No-one was answering. I had to get to the airport, but I couldn't leave my car on the side of the road. It was a clearway and it would get towed. There was one person I hadn't called—Fran. I had barely spoken to her in nearly two months and I wasn't sure whether she would answer, but I was that desperate I had to try.

Fran answered on the third ring. She sounded happy to hear from me and said she wouldn't mind waiting at the car. I had no idea why she was being so nice to me, but I didn't have a whole lot of time to think about it. I left the car unlocked with the keys in the ignition — it wasn't like anyone could steal it — and hailed a cab. When I was on the way to the airport I rang the insurance company and told them I was called away to an emergency and a friend was on her way to look after the car. Then I called Spencer.

'Morning', he said with a husky morning voice.

'Hi, I'm in a cab on the way to the airport', I said. 'O'Brien is apparently on his way to London. Is he allowed out of the country?'

'Since he won his appeal he can pretty much do as he pleases', Spencer replied. 'It would be good to ask him where he is headed and what the reason for the trip is so we can continue to build up our file on him. We haven't got very far. In fact, you'll need to call Margaret Black when you get back to the office to make another time to meet. Make sure you take note of who he is travelling with, by the way. He's a notorious womaniser.' And with that he said goodbye and hung up.

Spencer didn't sound as happy to hear from me as he usually did. Maybe he was in bed with someone? Maybe he wasn't happy with me? He obviously didn't think I was working hard enough because I hadn't followed up with Margaret Black. I had left a voicemail message for her, though, and the rest of my work time had been taken up being Spencer's lackey.

As soon as the taxi pulled up at the airport I threw the last $50 cash I had left before payday at the driver and raced into the international terminal. I had only seen photos of the elusive man in the newspaper, but my weeks of research ensured I knew exactly who I was looking for. I checked the departure times of all London-bound flights and the next one was due to leave at midday. It was

9 am, so it was safe to say I had probably beaten him to the airport.

I walked around the terminal, looking in every cafe and loitering outside every toilet with a clear view of the customs doors. If he was there I certainly couldn't see him. I called Janice to tell her I had arrived and gave her an update on the flight details. This was not a woman who wanted to engage in small talk.

'We know he's on his way. Just don't lose him, or else, Maggie', was Janice's only comment.

I had no idea what the 'or else' meant, but there was no way this man was going to cause me to lose my job. I walked as close to the customs doors as humanly possible without a passport and waited. He was so high profile he might have been taken through another entrance, but I couldn't worry about that.

There was a cafe to the left of customs and I was able to order a coffee and drink it while keeping a clear view of the international departures lounge. The girl who served me was from London and while I waited I found myself chatting to her about why she was working at the airport. How does someone fly halfway around the world for a holiday and end up working at a cafe in the international departures wing of an airport? I decided she must have been saving to go home and this was the best way to keep her motivated. Maybe I should change jobs and go to work in a bank?

At 11 am, just as I was starting to give up hope and the English girl was starting whine on, O'Brien walked through the Executive Club doors about 20 metres from the customs entrance. He was shepherding along a blonde who looked no older than me—she was definitely not his wife. I pulled out my phone and took as many photos as

I could as I raced up to him, put my dictaphone under his nose and demanded he tell me the reason he was heading overseas.

'No comment', he said.

Cocky bastard. I was not going to let him get away without saying anything on the record.

'You've ruined the life of hundreds of families and you still manage to act as though the world should bow to you. What do you have to say for yourself?'

'I was acquitted on all charges. Please leave me in peace', he said, smiling.

'Who's the blonde?' I shouted as he walked through the sliding doors into customs and out of my sight.

'My assistant', he said smugly as he patted her on the behind.

She was definitely not his assistant.

Adrenalin was pumping through my body. I'd got him. I couldn't believe it. I had finally seen O'Brien in the flesh. The way he stroked the young woman's backside made me shudder. Then I thought of his sister, Margaret. Now I could see why she wanted to air her grievances to the first journalist who bothered to track her down. Her brother was a Class A pig. I raced out of the airport, jumped in a cab, which I was going to have to get work to pay for, and called Spencer.

'I got him', I screamed excitedly down the phone.

'Well done, Maggie', he said.

I explained that he was with a blonde and that he had acted as though he didn't have a care in the world.

'Come back to the office so we can find out who the woman is.'

'I'll send you the photos from my phone', I said before I hung up.

I was beside myself with happiness; I had broken a story. I was certain the blonde wasn't O'Brien's assistant and if I was correct, I had just given *The City* a massive step towards discrediting him and letting the world know what a scumbag he was. Once I sent the photos I called Fran and thanked her profusely for saving my bacon with the car.

'Is the car okay?' I asked.

'Not exactly', she replied. 'It had to be towed to a mechanic. The guy thought there was something wrong with the engine. A belt was broken or something. I didn't understand what he was talking about to tell you the truth.'

She gave me details of the mechanic the car had been towed to and I thanked her again. Then I called the mechanic to find out how much I was going to have to fork out.

The car needed $700 worth of repairs. The mechanic, John, said I could try to get a better quote, but he guaranteed his was going to be the cheapest. I had paid off $1950 on my Universal credit card and with the $150 roadside mechanic fee and the car I was going to be backtracking $850. I really didn't want to spend $700 on the car, so I told him not to do anything to it until I had called him again. I had to get back to the office and find out who the woman with O'Brien was.

O'Brien's lady friend turned out to be the wife of O'Brien's lawyer, Jerry James. Spencer told me that Jerry was O'Brien's oldest friend and no-one seemed to know his wife, Haylee, had left him. By the time I made it back to the office, Spencer had already been in contact with Jerry and Mr O'Brien's wife, Kate, to get a comment about their partners' alleged affair. Neither was prepared to speak on the record, but Spencer said neither sounded surprised.

The next day my story was going to be on the front page of *The City* with EXCLUSIVE written next to my name. As I was going through one last edit of my copy, Spencer came over and asked me out for a drink with a few other people. I didn't have any spare cash until the next day when I got paid, but I wanted to see Spencer, so how could I say no? I would just use the credit card once more. It had been too big a day not to go out and celebrate.

The other people included Janice, who was all over Spencer like a rash, and a few colleagues. We were at a bar called Candle, which was attached to one of the best restaurants in the city. Genevieve and I sat at the bar talking to our colleagues and I felt like the champion of the world for catching O'Brien in the act. I tried not to notice the amount of airtime Spencer was giving my strange boss, but it seemed like they were old friends who had a lot of catching up to do.

I waited patiently at the bar with Genevieve, hoping Spencer would come over to talk to me, and while we waited it was champagne all round. The bartender kept refilling our glasses and we kept slugging them back. Then we ordered two Wagyu beef burgers the bar was famous for and devoured them, but still no Spencer. Genevieve didn't say a word about my obvious liking of my new colleague. She just sat next to me, kept the champagne flowing and bitched about Janice, while I suffered in silence.

Spencer may not have been paying me much attention, but Dave the creepy crime writer seemed to have forgotten the last time I had knocked him back. He had turned up at the bar about an hour after we had all arrived and was, to put it nicely, completely wasted. He had apparently been having a tough time at home since his wife had left and decided I was the woman to help him through it. I pretended to listen to his sob-story for about two minutes before turning back to Genevieve and getting on with the task at hand. When Genevieve excused herself a few minutes later to go to the ladies, Dave seized the opportunity and spun the stool I was sitting on around to face him.

At first I didn't know what he was doing. He was giving me a strange smile and I politely smiled back. I was about to turn back to my drink when I noticed his hands in a strange fan position near his crotch. I looked down and gasped. He had his pants unzipped and was about to expose himself to me. I was disgusted, to say the least. What kind of a person does that?

'What the hell are you doing? Zip up your pants', I seethed.

'I'm just trying to show you how much I like you', he said with slurred speech.

'Dave, do up your pants and go home', I heard Spencer shout from behind me.

'It's okay, Spencer. I've got this under control', I said. I didn't want Spencer to think I couldn't handle myself.

'But he was harassing you', Spencer said.

'I'm well aware of that', I replied. 'If you want to help, stop staring and get him out of here.'

Before we had a chance to get the drunken fool out of the building, Dave had fallen over and was spreadeagled on the floor. Spencer was forced to do up Dave's pants and escort him from the building and into a taxi.

Genevieve returned from the bathroom and asked why Spencer was walking with his arm around Dave. After I told her the story she admitted that Dave had tried the same tactic to win her heart when she first started at the paper.

'Are you all right? You look like you're in shock', Genevieve said, laughing.

Genevieve had such a warm Scottish lilt when she spoke, but her laugh was another thing altogether—she cackled. As soon as she started laughing, the shock of Dave's antics hit me and I was soon laughing so hard I also nearly fell off the stool. It was officially time to give up our posts and get the bill.

When the bartender handed over our docket, Genevieve immediately handed it back and said there must have been a mistake.

'No mistake', he said once he had examined it.

'What's wrong?' I asked.

Genevieve handed me the unassuming piece of paper and I felt the Wagyu burger lurch up my throat.

'What the hell? Two hundred and sixteen dollars!' I exclaimed.

The bartender said we had not asked to see a wine list when we sat down and asked for the champagne to keep flowing. So it wasn't his fault if we didn't know the only champagne the bar sold was $18 a glass.

At that moment the goddess of bad tidings, Janice, appeared out of nowhere with Spencer and a few other people behind her.

'What's wrong with you two?' she asked.

We were still too shocked about the bill to answer.

'We're just going to pay the bill and head home', Genevieve finally said.

I gave the bartender my Universal card and watched him key in $108 and press ENTER. Despite drinking six glasses of champagne, I was suddenly sober and did not want to be standing in a bar on a Tuesday night with

Janice or Spencer. I wanted to go home, get into bed and hope the evening had been nightmare.

'This cannot be happening to me. I'm broke again', I said to Genevieve as I slouched in the back of a cab.

'I know what you mean', she said.

I didn't think she did, though. I went to bed feeling terrible. I'd gone out and spent far more than I could afford and now I had the car repairs to contend with as well.

Lessons learned

- Analyse your spending – go through your credit card statements (and work out how much interest you're paying).
- Draw up a budget.
- Get up earlier so you can have breakfast at home and prepare lunch.
- Don't be a martyr. If you don't like cereal, don't buy it – have toast for breakfast instead.
- Set up a direct debit from your savings account to your credit card account.
- Check who you're sending an email to before you send it!
- Stay away from sleazy men named Dave.

PART III

Cold hard facts
23 April to 7 June

Universal credit card: $3800 owing
LAND credit card: $900 owing
Parking fines: $400
Happiness: frustrated

W hen you're broke, the hardest thing to hear is that there's more to life than money. I had a habit of every now and again spending like there was no tomorrow, as though it meant nothing, but I was a fraud. I really believed that money was essential to the modern existence, and when I woke up after my night on the town, nothing was going to make me forget the way my heart hammered in my chest when the bartender pushed the $216 tab across the bar. For a split second I thought I was having chest pains and was about to have a heart attack. In actual fact I had broken my own heart. This may have been a tad melodramatic, but sometimes shame is the only way to change.

My broken down car forced me to brave the elements and for the first time in months I walked to work, with a horrible hangover in tow. The five-kilometre trip across the city to the office took me about 50 minutes, of which I spent five minutes feeling nauseated from the six glasses of champagne I had consumed the night before and the other 45 minutes telling myself I would never be broke again. Not even seeing my hard-earned front-page story as I walked past newsstands could make up for the fact that I had drunk $108 worth of champagne, my car was going to cost $700 to get back on the road and most of my good work decreasing the debt on my Universal card was erased. It was embarrassing to think that a few glasses of good fizz had broken my bank and I had been stupid enough to trust a bartender to serve reasonably priced booze.

As I walked I was determined to change my fortune. I felt like Scarlett O'Hara returning home to her beloved Tara after the civil war in *Gone with the Wind* and proclaiming to the universe that she would never, ever, go hungry again. 'I will never be broke again', I repeated over and over. At one point I got so into my mantra I even raised my fist into the air, which must have made me look like a complete weirdo to passengers on the bus that was passing at the exact same moment.

Seeing my name on the front page of *The City* should have made me feel elated, especially considering it had come on the back of weeks and weeks of sitting in a car watching O'Brien's apartment and several more searching the archives at the library. As much as my story shamed O'Brien, glory didn't seem so important anymore. It had taken me months to pay off a decent chunk of my credit card and all of a sudden I was backtracking. I had to keep going, I couldn't lose confidence in myself. And besides, I was a professional when it came to financial disasters and I was going to turn my fortune around if it killed me.

In the past the thought of not having a car for a few weeks would have been enough to whip me into action to get some funds together, most likely by increasing my credit card limit, so that the rest of my life was not disturbed in any way. This time I was going to go out of my way to act responsibly and deal with the repercussions of only having a limited amount of cash.

I had arrived in the office more than an hour before I was scheduled to start and rather than reading the news online, I decided to take action and ring around some mechanics to find one who could fix my car for less than the $700 the mechanic John had quoted. Although he had seemed like an honest person, I was not going to rest until I found a cheaper workshop to fix my car. I had to ring him first, though, to find out the correct terminology to describe what was actually wrong with the car so I didn't sound like a complete idiot when I started ringing random businesses. He was pretty nice about it and he said if I found a better offer he would match it.

And I was off. It took me 60 minutes and about 20 phone calls to mechanics in every part of the city for me to find a man who said he could repair my car for $500. I rang back John and he didn't renege on his deal. He said he would start the repairs that morning, but it would be at least 10 days before the car was ready because he had to order a part from Germany. As far as I was concerned he could keep the car for a month—I'd saved myself $200. It was payday and I still had $622 in my savings account for rent, food and bills once the $150 was taken out for the Universal card. There was not going to be a cent spent on anything else, not even the hot chips I was craving to cure my hangover.

As was the story of my life, there was another problem to contend with: the parking fines I still hadn't paid. I knew they would be accumulating late fee after late fee, I just didn't know the best way to tackle them. So I did what I did best and decided to leave them until I was sent another letter. Smart thinking 99.

When I finally looked up to find Genevieve, the first person I laid eyes on was Dave. I had put his strip show out of my mind as soon as my head hit the pillow the night before and didn't want to have to talk to him. He was pathetic, rude and I pitied him for being so desperate he would try it on with someone who had previously let him know she just wasn't interested. His bizarre pick-up technique was, without a doubt, the most cringe-worthy act I had ever witnessed, and the thought of having to sit within 10 metres of his desk conjured up fantasies of quitting my job.

Dave didn't seem to remember his drunken shenanigans and walked straight up to my desk with a copy of the paper, pointed to the photo I had taken of O'Brien and his mistress splashed across the front page and said, 'What a legend'. Dave was charm personified.

'Did you have a good night?' I asked, trying to embarrass him enough that he would never dare cross the newsroom floor and disturb me ever again.

'Brilliant', he replied. 'Went to a bar called Candle, you probably wouldn't know it, and picked up a nice little blonde journalist from *The Tome*. Great night all round.'

I couldn't believe my ears. He was so full of crap. There was no way I was going to tell him what he'd actually gotten up to the night before, I wanted him to find out for himself when the memory filtered back into his consciousness and made him flinch with pain. I also wanted his pudgy face out of my sight; however, it seemed he had one last tasty morsel for me to relish.

'Did you hear about Janice and Spencer? Appears they finally got together.'

'Finally? He's only been here a month.'

I couldn't believe what I was hearing. A small part of me really thought Spencer liked me.

'They've been flirting from afar for years. Her divorce seems to have put them back on track.'

'Dave, it's 9 am for goodness sake, do you think I really want to hear about my colleagues' romantic escapades?'

I could hear the defensive tone of my voice and feel my cheeks flushing. Spencer was too nice for her. What was he doing? Then, out of nowhere, I thought I was going to cry. What was wrong with me? It must have been the hangover.

'I need something to eat', I said, walking off in the direction of the kitchen and bathrooms before he could say anything else to me.

It couldn't be true. Dave didn't know what he was talking about. The man couldn't even remember almost flashing me the night before. My crush was crushed. I was so disappointed in Spencer's choice in women that I vowed to wipe him from my mind. First the money and then the man; it was a day of vows.

I knew there wasn't anything romantic going on between Spencer and me, just a little bit of harmless flirting over our O'Brien research. It was just that after my horror relationship with Guy, I was a little gun-shy and knew I could have made myself more available to Spencer. Instead, I was a tad rude to the one person, apart from Genevieve, I actually liked at my job and who had allowed me to work on something for the first time in months outside the pleather interiors of the work motor vehicles. On the face of things, though, if he was going to chase after someone like Janice, there wasn't much point worrying.

As I sat down at my desk there was a message pending on my screen. I opened my email and, low and behold, the message was from Janice. It seemed that I couldn't get away from that woman.

'You did such great work at the airport, I'd like you to go back on stake-out at O'Brien's city penthouse. It will be an ongoing assignment until Jack or Kate O'Brien talks to you', she wrote.

I wrote back a polite 'No problem' and turned off my computer so I could leave before my urge to massacre both Dave and Janice overtook me. Then I came to my senses and remembered O'Brien was in London. Why on earth was she sending me back out there? This was clearly a backhanded comment and she just wanted me out of the office. I started to walk towards her desk, saw her slam down the phone and thought it best to do as she had asked without making a fuss.

As I was heading to the stairs to go and get a work car I heard Spencer calling my name from his cubicle. Ah great, I thought. After Janice, he was the second-last person I wanted to talk to. On the other hand, he was the only person who would know why I was being sent on a wild-goose chase, so I thought there was no harm in seeing what he wanted.

I could see his head peeking around the side of his workspace. Even with a hangover he looked handsome.

'Fun night last night, wasn't it? Except for Dave's antics I mean', he said as I stopped at his desk and lent over the partition to see him.

'Yeah, fun', I replied less enthusiastically. What the hell was he talking about? I was harassed and stuck with a $108 tab, and now I also had to figure out how to pay for my broken car.

'Are you heading out for the day or are you going to be around so we can discuss O'Brien? We could have lunch?' Spencer suggested.

I thought it a touch strange that he would want to have lunch with me rather than with his new lover. He was such a hard worker, it seemed not even a woman could tear him away from what he was working on.

'I'm back on O'Brien stake-out duty. By the way, do you know why I'm being sent to his place if we know he's in London?'

'Janice must be in a bad mood. She got pretty drunk last night and got a little wild', he said, laughing his gravelly laugh. 'I'll have a chat to her if you like. I might just be able to use my influence to get her to change her mind.'

I told him not to worry about talking to Janice and that I would call Margaret Black when I was out on the road. I didn't want to upset Janice any more than she already was and I certainly didn't want Spencer using his love connection with her to help me at work.

'You could also try to get his wife to talk', he said, scribbling down her number out of his contacts book.

Spencer was right. If I could get hold of Kate O'Brien and convince her to tell her side of the saga before her husband flew back into the country, I would have another great story. As soon as I exited the car park, I phoned Margaret Black to see if I could visit her. I had called her several times since our one and only meeting, but she hadn't returned my calls, which seemed odd considering she was so open with me. I was undeterred. I needed to know more about her brother's dealings at Shamrock Enterprises. That, I decided, was the key to the story. She had mentioned the fallout with Shamrock and I had a gut feeling she knew more than anyone thought she did.

Margaret didn't answer her phone, so I left a message asking her to call me as soon as she was available. When I called Kate O'Brien a recorded voice said the number was no longer in use. Someone doesn't want to be contacted, I said to myself. Who did I think I was? Columbo? I was starting to talk to myself in detective-speak.

I arrived at the O'Brien's apartment block to see Kate walking into the building with a dog in tow. I didn't have time to open the car door before she was inside, where she remained for the rest of the day.

The next day she took the dog for a walk in the morning again and when she returned I was waiting for her, but her doorman pushed me out the way so I couldn't get near her.

By the third day Kate's routine was clear. At 10 am she left her building in a velour tracksuit with her giant German Shepherd and headed to the track around the botanical gardens, opposite the apartment building.

Rather than sitting around waiting for her, I decided to walk as well. My pants were getting tighter by the day and if I didn't watch out I would have to start worrying about buying new clothes to compensate for my expanding waistline. At 9.30 am I ran over to the toilets in the park, changed into my leggings, T-shirt and runners, and waited for Kate to appear, then I followed her around the walking path as she took her daily turn. She was obviously very fit, powering along, and I was never in any danger of catching up to her. It definitely beat being in the office or working out at the gym.

As we neared the end of her six-kilometre circuit, I ran ahead and waited for her to turn towards home, but she surprised me and went into a cafe. I thought if I waited outside until she came out I could avoid scaring her. Instead I basically jumped out of nowhere and gave her a near heart attack, making her spill her coffee down her white Stella McCartney gym outfit. Who the hell wore Stella McCartney for a walk anyway?

I ran up to her when she walked out of the cafe a few minutes later with a new coffee and introduced myself.

As soon as the words *The City* came out of my mouth she turned and walked away from me.

'Mrs O'Brien, I've been sent here to talk to you', I said, walking after her. 'Can you comment on your husband's alleged affair?'

'Please leave me alone. I have nothing to say', she replied.

Despite fobbing me off Kate continued to walk and get her coffee each morning, so that was what I did too. I tried to talk to her every day and each time she said, 'No comment'. When I told Janice I was having no luck she just said to keep trying.

To save money I had forbidden myself from more than one takeaway coffee each day. I loved coffee as much as the next person and if I had been in the office I would have had no problem having a quick cup of instant, fresh from the not-so-fresh container in the office's kitchen. So, even though the idea of drinking a thermos of stagnant instant coffee went against ever fibre of my being, it was what I started to do.

Once I had the coffee situation under control, I came up with a plan to stop buying lunch too. I realise that the concept of walking into a cafe and only ordering coffee may sound like a ridiculously easy challenge, but when it came to cafe-style food, I was not a normal person and my weight and my wallet were not going to be helped by my penchant for delicious food to accompany a freshly aerated skinny latte.

The first day I tried out my plan was a struggle to say the least. The cafes near the O'Brien's penthouse were some of the best in the city. I longed to order the $15 meatball and mozzarella wrap, $10 avocado bruschetta or $12 prosciutto and asiago cheese panini on offer at one of them.

As I sat in the car, bored and hungry, I told myself making my lunch every day would not only help me save, it would also make me the Nigella Lawson of my own home. It would mean that for 10 minutes while I constructed a sandwich filled with poached chicken, dill, cucumber, spinach and mayonnaise on multigrain bread that I, Maggie Rose, was a sultry culinary siren who could make men pant with unadulterated desire after watching me lick my fingers as though I was taste testing a warm chocolate ganache pudding. I may have been single, with no romantic prospects, and living with my best friend, but there was no reason for me not to be a domestic goddess cooking wonderful food and saving money while I was at it.

Amazingly my lunch plan was working, although it took a hell of a lot of strength. By the first week of May I discovered I had some semblance of the foreign notion people call willpower.

Everything seemed to be falling into place. Eliza had kept her promise and stayed out of my way as I waded through my own version of the global financial crisis and I loved her dearly for it. There was one minor hiccup, however. One Sunday morning I woke up after being out quite late the night before and was craving a gourmet breakfast. I checked the cupboards to see what I could have on toast and the only thing I could find was some apricot jam I had made the year before, the last time I had channelled Nigella. I was up for cracking open the jar, but, alas, there was no bread.

I tossed up whether to walk to the bakery and buy a $3 loaf of wholemeal, but me being me, I nipped into our local cafe to pick up something else. I chose a freshly made chicken, avocado and cos lettuce sandwich with tzatziki and preserved lemon, and a coffee. I had the house to myself, so as I walked back past the video store I had recently joined I hired a new release to watch while I read the papers. It was going to be a blissful, lazy Sunday. That was until Eliza and Tom came home.

I had just sat down to tuck into my sandwich when I heard a key in the front door. I don't know why, but I panicked. A sudden attack of guilt took over and I thought if Eliza caught me eating the sandwich instead of muesli or toast, World War III would erupt. I didn't have time to run to the kitchen and put the sandwich in the fridge, so I stuffed it behind me on the couch.

Eliza and Tom came straight into the lounge room to say hello and I felt paralysed with fear they would discover the store-bought sandwich, which was now starting to seep through my T-shirt. Then the unthinkable happened—they sat down to watch the movie I had on. It had only just started when they walked in, so I was forced to sit through two hours and five minutes of Cameron Diaz while mayonnaise and preserved lemon dripped down my back and into my pants. As soon as the film finished Tom and Eliza said they were heading out again. When they had finally left, I stood up and the sandwich was stuck to my bottom. Oh happy day. After I had wiped all traces of mayonnaise off the leather couch I walked straight into the kitchen and ate a bowl of Eliza's fancy roasted, organic farm-bred muesli, just to annoy her.

The video store was the latest addition in my mission to live thin. I was still going out more than I should have been, so to entice myself to stay in I joined the local store, which turned out to be a veritable cinema wonderland. The first time I walked through the store's doors I was there for an hour before I settled on season one of *The West Wing*. It was a series I had wanted to watch for years and I figured it would keep me off the streets and on the straight and narrow for a few nights at least. And as I had to walk past the video store on my way to work, I couldn't see how it was going to be possible for me to get a single late fee.

My track record when it came to returning DVDs had never been flash and I had been blacklisted from the last place I was a member. A year earlier I had received a solicitor's letter from a video store demanding I return *Breathless*, the 1983 Richard Gere film I mistakenly rented instead of the 1960 Jean-Luc Godard French New Wave film with the same title. I had rented it purely to impress Guy, who had said he had studied it during his arts degree. Needless to say my ego took a beating when he corrected my mistake.

The bloody film ended up costing me $300 in late fees, including $150 to the store's solicitor. I had gone to Eliza with the legal letter and, between fits of hysterical laughter, she advised me to pay up. Without me knowing, she kept the letter and hung it in our bathroom to keep me in line.

My biggest problem curbing my efforts to save was not the food or the fines. Despite my new video store regime, I still had a severe disdain for staying in at night. Since I was 17 and had started sneaking out to nightclubs I had not been able to stay away from the lure of a good night out. This was not to say I frequented seedy bars on the hunt for men. I just had a lot of friends who liked to be out and about rather than watching television on a weeknight. For me, trying to stay in when someone had invited me to catch up at a nice restaurant or gallery opening was akin to asking an alcoholic if they wanted another glass of wine.

About a week later as I walked back to my car after my daily walk and coffee—I had stopped stalk-walking Mrs O'Brien and changed my walk time to later in the day to avoid any kind of contact that could lead to police prosecution and a restraining order—Spencer was standing next to my car. As usual, he looked great, while I was in leggings and an old U2 concert tour T-shirt I had owned for more 15 years. His arms were crossed and I could see his strong forearms and biceps. I was hoping he wouldn't notice my growing thighs.

Why did he have to be going out with Janice? And when did I start paying attention to men's arms? I thought as I approached him.

'What are you doing here? Have you come to replace me?' I asked hopefully. God, I wanted to be back in the office more than I ever thought possible. I would have happily gone and sat next to Dave if it meant I could leave the bloody car.

'I was just passing by and thought I'd come and see how you were going. So, how are you going?'

'As good as can be expected; nothing much happening here. Kate only leaves the house for her morning walk, as far as I can tell, and there's been no sign of the husband.'

'How about a coffee then? I'll buy', he said.

I had no idea why Spencer had come to see me. He couldn't have just dropped by. It was very odd and a severe case of micro-management was springing to mind. Then I started to get paranoid. Was he checking up on me? There was no other reason for him to stop by. I had been on the stake-out for weeks and weeks and still hadn't come up with anything. Was my failure to produce being talked about at the office? Were he and Janice conspiring against me?

I took him to a different cafe from the one I usually went to in case Kate O'Brien came in and was scared off. I had calmed down by the time our coffees arrived and was ready to hear what he had to say. Instead of a stern talk, Spencer told me about chasing Jack O'Brien for more than 18 months after he had been tipped off about O'Brien's dodgy dealings. The more he dug, he said, the more he found out about O'Brien's illegal business operations and just how many people were being ripped off.

'He didn't care who he took money from: prime ministers, banking executives, private hospitals, charities, mum and dad investors who had their whole retirement funds wrapped up in his schemes, and single mums. They were all taken for a ride. As long as people had the cash to invest, he wasn't worried about the morality involved with stealing it. I called the police as soon as I figured out he was siphoning off billions of dollars to offshore bank accounts in tax-free havens all around the globe, rather than a few million botched investments I initially thought I was dealing with.'

As he talked, I sat there going all googly eyed. This man was a champion. He was Robin Hood, sans tights. I found myself thinking about how strong his arms and hands were, before I pulled myself together and concentrated on what he was saying. After Spencer had finished talking about O'Brien, he said he wanted to know about me. I told him a mini version of my life prior to joining *The City* and tried to change the subject back to him. He was more interesting than any man I had met in a long time, if ever.

Spencer said he was the oldest of five children. He finished an economics degree, then decided he wanted to be a journalist. Like me he travelled for a year or so before he started working full-time. He said although journalists were increasingly getting a bad name for having flimsy morals, he wanted to be part of something where the truth was told and the bastards were kept honest. I could smell a leftie with my eyes closed; Spencer and I were cut from the same cloth.

'So what's next then for O'Brien?' I asked, trying to ignore the thoughts of kissing him that had raced back into my head.

'What do you do with yourself when you're not running around being an ace reporter?' he asked, ignoring my question.

Now I had no idea what he was doing. Had he come out to check on me or chat me up?

'I share a house with my friend Eliza', I replied.

Just when I was about to start reluctantly opening up, his phone rang and he said he had to get back to the office. Perfect timing. I was off the hook, mind the pun.

'You're doing a good job, Maggie. I don't want you to think you're forgotten out here. I'll keep you updated a bit more often from now on. I have to get back to the office, but I just wanted to make sure you were okay.'

'Thanks, I'd better get back to the car', I said, as once again my face became hot and flushed.

I can't think about this man anymore, I said to myself as he drove off. I had far greater things to worry about than an unrequited crush.

As soon as I got home I went into Eliza's room to tell her about Spencer's bizarre fly-by visit.

'So what do you think? Was he checking up on me or trying to chat me up?' I asked.

'Definitely trying to woo you. That's exciting. Do you like him?' Eliza said.

'He's very handsome and sweet, but I'd never do anything about it and, to tell you the truth, I think he was checking up on me. He's with Janice anyway.'

'As I always say, "If he doesn't have a ring on his finger, he's anybody's".'

What could I say—Eliza was a madwoman.

It was Friday afternoon on 15 May and I had been told I was officially off the O'Brien stake-out and I would be back in the office on Monday. I was so relieved I wanted nothing more than to head to a bar and meet up with my friends for a few relaxing drinks, followed by dinner somewhere. As hitting the town was not part of my savings plan I decided to call my friend Grace, and invite her out for a 'cheap and cheerful' dinner. As soon as I had invited her I started to panic and question exactly what we should do. After an hour of fretting I decided that if I could make my lunch and avoid the food I lusted after at lunchtime every day, I could at least try to hold back on spending much on a night out.

My initial plan was to spend only $30 on dinner and a few drinks, then catch public transport home. When I had showered, changed and was ready to head back into town to meet Grace, my old habits came flying back. Should I just take a taxi rather than catch a train? Maybe I could increase my allowance to $50? Then the willpower I had recently discovered came to life again. No, I would do what I had planned.

Once I had walked the 10 minutes to the station, jumped on a train and gone the six stops to central station I was very happy with myself. I took the time on the train to go over the 'stay and go' list I had made in January to see if I had made much progress. I could see I was a little green behind the ears when I wrote the plan. As far as the 'go' side was concerned I had come a fair way. I had stopped getting regular blow-waves, which should have been saving me more than $100 a month, and had gone back to the daily battle with my round brush. Eliza and I were buying cheaper by the dozen boxes of wine once a month and, despite the setback with my car, I had made great progress on the Universal credit card—I had paid off close to $2000. Go me!

Stay	Go
• Regular haircut and dye	• Going out so often
• Dumpling dinners with Max and Jem	• Credit cards
	• ~~Weekly blow-waves~~
• ~~Gym membership~~	• ~~Driving to work~~
• Good-quality food	• ~~Expensive wine (could buy cheaper)~~
• ~~Living with Fran and Tim~~	• ~~Breakfast at work every day~~
• Books	• Occasional drunken cigarettes
• ~~Weekly swims~~	
• Car	

I decided on dinner at a pub that we had been regulars at as students. Not a week went by when one of us hadn't dropped in for a game of pool and a drink following lectures, or during, as was often the case. In our university days it was known for serving stock-standard bar food and cheap drinks. It had since become a gastropub, and as I walked through the salon-style doors I could not believe how much it had changed. Gone were the manky couches and pool tables, and in their place were leather benches and a stunning dimmed dining area with an incredible silver wallpaper embossed with a white paisley print, and flickering candles on each table.

Grace was already there, sitting at a table with a bottle of red and two glasses. Shit, paying for half a bottle of wine was definitely not part of my plan, I thought.

'I bought us a bottle to celebrate', Grace said as I sat down.

'Celebrate what?' I asked.

'My paper has a new bureau opening in New York and I've been asked to go over and be one of the correspondents.'

'That's amazing. Congratulations!'

'I'm so ready to get out of this place. I've never left the country and I've been desperate to see the world ever since you packed up and left when we finished university. I'll never forget how jealous I was of you.'

I was so relieved she had bought the wine I immediately sat down and drank the first glass in about 30 seconds flat. We talked about her move, our work and then I mentioned Spencer's visit, expecting Grace to agree that it was strange for a colleague to drop in on a stake-out.

'Spencer's lovely', Grace said.

'How do you know him?' I asked, sounding a little jealous.

'You're a classic, Maggie', she said laughing. 'He went out with one of the columnists at work for two years and he used to drink with us on Friday nights. What's he done to you?'

'Nothing, really. I just can't work out whether he likes me or whether he's trying to keep me in line.'

'Give him a go, Maggie. When I heard he was working at *The City* I thought you two would hit it off on day one.'

I wanted Spencer to be a good person. He had stood up for me when Dave unzipped his pants and had offered to get me off stake-out duty. Still, if he was now dating Janice he must have had a major character flaw Grace had not seen.

Reigning in the spending on the dinner was easier than I thought it was going to be. Despite the stylish surrounds, the food was reasonably priced and the pizza I ordered was only $10. I told Grace I thought it was going to be totally overpriced.

'I'm saving like crazy to get out of debt', I said as though this was something Grace and I would normally talk about.

'Yeah, I heard you had a spot of trouble with Tim and Fran. Or is this more to do with your Saturn change thing Max was talking about at Eliza's birthday dinner?' Grace asked.

'Bloody hell, everybody seems to know about my money matters', I replied, a little annoyed. 'Despite what you may have heard, I didn't leave on bad terms. I do need to catch up with them soon, though, I haven't seen either of them since I left and Fran did me a huge favour recently when my car broke down.'

After we had finished dinner and the bottle of red, Grace suggested another bottle. That was when another foreign concept came into my head. I told her I was actually ready to go home and have an early night.

'Maggie Rose, I'm impressed', Grace said, smiling.

As I sat on the train I had never been prouder of myself, not even when I had got the job at *The City*. I'd done it: I had spent only $10 on the pizza and had told Grace that next time I would buy her a bottle of red.

I took matters further the next day when I went to a bookshop and bought two of the latest personal finance self-help books, designed for people wanting to sort out their money matters and get ahead. My mother would have been so proud. I then went home to read them. One of the books was going to tell me how to clear my credit card debt and save money. The other understood the trials and tribulations women face as their 20s come to a close.

I chose the first book because the cover appealed to me; it had a picture of a pair of black Converse high-tops filled with cash. In my haste to get home and consume the information I didn't even look at the title, and when I started reading I soon realised it was more of an invest-ment guide than a savings manual. In fact, on about the third page of the introduction it said, 'This is not a book about the basics of savings'. Even though I knew it wasn't what I specifically needed, I kept reading and it turned out to be very interesting, and, if I'd had any money to begin with, it would have been a good place to start to make some more. The author talked about risk profiles (I didn't seem to fit into any of the categories, but if there was a high-risk category I could have slotted right in) and inflation: apparently if my $4500-odd credit card debt was a savings figure it would have been worth a whole lot more in 20 years' time.

One thing that stuck in my mind as my eyes scanned the pages of the risk chapter was the risk I would take if I didn't do anything at all. The author said the biggest risk is accepting that what you have is your lot in life. I didn't want to be a 65-year-old woman getting by week to week on her pension, just as I was doing as a 29 year old. The thought of having to rely on the government to eat and sleep was even more depressing than having a credit card debt. By the time I'd finished the chapter I was anxious to get some money in the bank to go towards my first home and get me some collateral, otherwise I was going to be in Eliza's spare room forever.

When I moved on to the second book I was hyper-ventilating every time I thought of my debt. The book was aimed at helping women get rich, and sounded too good to be true. Again, the stark reality of living on a pension was laid bare to scare the living daylights out of the reader. Could I really live on $335 a week if I were to find myself alone and without any savings for the future when I retire? Judging by the way I spent money now, it was highly unlikely. Of course, my generation (I was either an X or a Y depending on my mood) had been contributing to their super funds since they started working, something our forbearers never had a chance to do because mandatory employer superannuation contri-butions weren't introduced until the early 1990s.

As per the author's explicit instructions I wrote down the things I wanted most in the world. This was something everyone was capable of doing.

Things I want most in the world

1 No debt
2 $10000 savings
3 My own home
4 A new car
5 The latest pair of Miu Miu shoes

If I had all these things, I would be truly happy, I thought after I had written them all down. The author said these were the goals to work towards and it was no good dreaming, I had to make my dreams a reality to be a truly worthwhile human being. I did want all the things I had written down; who didn't want their own home and savings? I just didn't share the writer's optimism that it was achievable.

I kept reading and within the first couple of chapters the message was plain and simple: my debts had to go before I could even consider starting to save for the house or the $10000. I was told to rank my debts from the highest to the lowest interest on each card and get rid of the biggest debt first. That was still my Universal card. I was to allocate the maximum amount of cash I could spare each month to go towards paying off the card. This probably meant more than the $150 a week I was already paying off, but I just wasn't sure how much I could afford. I kept reading to find out if the author told me the amount I should pay.

One of the examples put forward was widening the gap between hair appointments. I had very long hair that needed to be cut and dyed on a regular basis. It was a structured routine that had taken my hairdresser and me years to perfect. My hair was my crowning glory and there was just no way I was going to mess with it. I would be saving money, but a good haircut was essential. I had already given up the weekly blow-waves and gone back to the battle with the blow dryer.

Another hint to save was to eat less. There was no doubt in my mind this was something I needed to do as within two years I had put on more than seven kilograms. Fewer takeaway meals, fewer restaurant meals and less wine were all recommended. My job didn't involve any kind of vigorous exercise, 99 per cent of my time was spent at a desk and, despite walking six kilometres daily while staking out Kate O'Brien, my clothes didn't seem to be getting any more comfortable. I was feeling better, though — less drinking and more exercise seemed to agree with my mind.

My tight pants turned my attention from saving to the luxe clothes I wanted to buy from the latest issue of *Vogue*, another expense I was not willing to budge on. I hadn't purchased a single item of clothing for almost three months. This was something of a record and coupled with stopping the blow-waves, making my lunch and going out half as often, I should have saved thousands of dollars, not just the $2000 I had paid off my Universal card. There was also the monthly $500 rent I was saving since moving in with Eliza, but I had no idea where that had gone. I decided that before I could finish reading the book I had a vital question to answer: if I was spending less, how could I still be broke? I needed to find out where the rest of my money was going.

***

After spending a Saturday afternoon window shopping—this should be known as self-flagellation for the saver—I arrived to home find Eliza cooking an impromptu dinner party. She had decided our friends were acting far too grown up and we needed a night of debauchery and tasty food to bring us all down to earth. Tom was there, of course, as well as Grace, Max, Jem, Fran and Tim. I nearly cried with joy when my old housemates walked through the door. I had not laid eyes on either of them since I moved out of our home and seeing them again made my heart break for making them so upset with me. I had also neglected to properly thank Fran for helping me out with my car.

For the first hour there was a nonstop battle for people to get a word in. Max, as always, had something to say and say first, Tim and Tom were winding Max up and the girls tried to catch up on the parts of each other's lives we had missed since Eliza's birthday three months earlier. While we were all talking, Eliza whipped up spaghetti marinara and we sat around the table eating olives and artichokes and drinking red wine; it was heaven.

Fran and Tim were sitting either side of me. They told me about their new housemate and they both said they missed me. Fran loved her new job but hated the crap pay, and Tim said he was only a couple months off leaving his job and starting his own cafe. Yvette, his boss, was going to back him and I still wondered whether that was all she was doing. As I hadn't seen him in months I thought it rude to ask such a personal question.

As soon as I saw them I promised myself that not a word about money would come out of my mouth. I still found it quite painful to think of the psychological mess I got myself into when I didn't pay the rent and I didn't want any bad feelings to be revisited. I didn't need to worry though, as they were both desperate to find out what had happened with Janice and work since I had moved out. I gave them every gory detail, including the night out in the bar when Spencer tried to rescue me from Dave, my full-time job tailing the intercontinental Jack O'Brien and his wife, and Spencer's recent strange visit to my car. When I had finished prattling on I looked up to see the whole table was listening to me.

'Before anyone says anything, yes, she likes this Spencer character, she just doesn't want to admit it', Eliza said.

'I knew it', Grace said.

Luckily, the forever-faithful Fran stood up and shouted, 'Anyone for vodka?' We may not have seen each other much recently, but after living together for 18 months she still knew when I was getting uncomfortable.

Eliza went to pull out the bottle of Absolut frozen from the bottom of the freezer, and while Fran poured the drinks Max decided to steer the conversation towards his favourite drunken topic: the Saturn Return. He hadn't talked about it in months and, apart from when Grace had mentioned it at our recent dinner, the concept had completely slipped my mind.

'How is your year of transition going, Maggie? Have you made much progress on the money front?' he asked.

'You know how to pick your timing, Max', I replied. 'As a matter of fact I'm doing quite well. I've paid just over $2000 off one of my cards.'

'That's impressive, Maggie. What's your savings strategy?'

'I've set up a direct debit that transfers a set amount on payday from my savings account to my credit card. It's working, but it's slow', I admitted. I knew I should have been proud of myself, but I was not yet reformed and was scared I was still capable of tipping back into mega-debt territory.

'I hide all my money around the house. It's the only way I can stop myself from spending because I usually forget where I've put it', Grace said.

'I actually put my credit card in the freezer once', Eliza chimed in.

And before I knew it my five best friends were telling me the secrets of their savings success. Max and Jem said they moved into Max's parents' house to save for their first home because they didn't want to give up their busy social life. In the year they spent in Max's mum and dad's bungalow they saved the deposit for their first home. Tim said he had paid off his debts by living only on his credit card and paying it off with his entire pay cheque every fortnight.

My financial problems just seemed to blurt out of my mouth. I went on for at least half an hour about how I envied them all because, despite the small gains I'd made, I didn't seem to have it in me to be able to pay off my cards and I knew I should be clearing them quicker. I just didn't know how. Fran suggested I transfer the balance of my Universal card onto a card with a lower interest rate so I wasn't paying as much.

'Can I really do that?' I asked excitedly.

'Sure you can. Just find a low-interest-rate credit card and when you apply you can ask to transfer the balance from your old card to the new card. Then you can close the old card and just be left paying the new lower repayments', Fran explained.

The day after the impromptu dinner I decided to follow Fran's advice and look into transferring the balance of my Universal card. I was paying about 19 per cent interest. I'd had the card for years and initially only applied because it was attached to a frequent flyer program. At the time I was 24 and hell-bent on travelling overseas and it seemed like a good way to help me get there. How wrong I was. I had never used a single point towards a flight. I probably had thousands unused.

I found a consumer website dedicated to comparing every credit card in the country. I had no idea there were so many cards on offer. I went straight to the section on low-interest cards and looked at what each of them had to offer. I decided the best card for me was going to be a Wealth credit card, which had six months' interest free on purchases, balance transfers and an interest rate of only 11 per cent thereafter. It was practically the same as the LAND card I had applied for in December, but I went through with the application process and when I came to the financial page I included the $3350 I owed on the Universal card to transfer. The new card had a $4000 limit and I decided if I was accepted I would ask to have it decreased.

A week later, without any other contact from the bank, my new Wealth credit card arrived in the mail. My application had been accepted. I was over the moon. I was finally able to close my Universal credit card account. I couldn't believe I hadn't done a balance transfer to begin with. The only thing that really bothered me was the ease of getting the card. It was one of the big five banks, so I had no reason not to trust its credit services, but I hadn't even received an email telling me my application was pending. This was starting to feel all too familiar. The

LAND card was just as easy to receive and look where that had got me.

A couple of days later I walked into a branch of the Universal Bank and proudly told the teller I was there to close an account. However, the teller had some bad news for me: no money had been transferred from the Universal account to the Wealth Bank account. I called the Wealth Bank and the call centre operator said the balance had not been transferred because the amount I requested was too high. The bank had still kindly sent me the card without informing me. The operator said I could give over-the-phone permission to transfer a lower amount. I told them to transfer the maximum amount of $3000. That left me with $350 to pay off the Universal card before I could close it. I had only $200 in my savings account, so I would have to wait until payday.

I left the bank with the intention of going home and working out how I was going to juggle the repayments on the three cards. It shouldn't take me long to pay off the Universal card. And there didn't seem to be too much harm in having a third card, I thought. At least some of my debt would be paid off at a lower interest rate.

As I was walking home I stopped for a coffee. While I was waiting I absent-mindedly read the holiday deals on the travel agent's window next door. It had a sale on flights to Asia. I was yet to buy my ticket for Max and Jem's wedding so I thought there could be no harm in simply finding out what were the best deals on offer.

An hour later I walked out with a return flight to Kuala Lumpur, two transfers and seven nights' accommodation at the hotel Max and Jem had told everyone to book into. The entire transaction cost about $1500 and I put it all on my Universal card. This was for half the flight and a week's accommodation. The travel agent was able to access my frequent flyer records and I had enough points for a one-way ticket to Malaysia—perfect. As I watched the agent process my payment on the Universal credit card, I promised myself I wouldn't feel bad about paying for the trip because I had to get to the wedding somehow—I couldn't miss the big day. There were ways and means I could pay it off, I thought. Maybe I could get a second job and work on Sundays? Never going to happen.

By the time I got home Eliza was already there. She had left work early because she was going away with Tom for a week. I walked straight into her room and told her about my amazing deal on the flight and accommodation for the wedding trip to Malaysia.

'I don't mean to dampen your high spirits, but weren't you saying last week how bad your finances are? How can you afford to pay for the tickets now?' Eliza asked.

I couldn't. And even though I had promised myself I was able to justify buying the ticket, as soon as Eliza brought up my finances I was overcome with guilt and started to cry.

'I need help', I blubbered. 'I have no idea what I'm doing. I don't know why I bought the tickets. I tried to transfer the balance on my biggest debt to a new card and they sent me the card even though I had asked to rollover too much. I went to the bank to try to sort it out and they said I could only move across $3000. I did that, then went and spent another $1500 on my old card anyway.'

'You're right, you do need help. I didn't want to say anything to you because I could see you were trying so hard, but I'm going to say it now. It's the start of June—in a few months you're turning 30. You have to get your shit together, Maggie.'

'I know. Everything I've tried has turned out to be a disaster. I seriously think I have some kind of illness and I'm going to be in debt for the rest of my life. I'm so sick of worrying about money. I'm so ashamed of myself—all I want is to be a normal person who's able to sustain some semblance of willpower. I thought I was doing well and I was so excited when Fran told me about transferring my balance. I never thought it would get me into a worse situation than I was already in.'

'You don't have an illness and you have to seriously start taking responsibility for your actions', Eliza said. 'I think some proper guidance would not go astray at this point. You might find this hard to believe, but I know what you're going through. Throughout my entire law degree I lived on credit and kept increasing my limit to get myself through. By the time I had finished I had a $12 000 debt.'

'I had no idea', I said, shocked at my friend's admission. 'Why didn't you tell me?'

'I was deeply ashamed and you know what I'm like. I was in a pretty bad place.'

'What did you do?' I couldn't believe what I was hearing. Eliza was, without a doubt, the most sensible and hardworking person I knew. The idea that she could have been in a worse situation than me was simply unfathomable.

'I'd just started my articles and was getting paid a proper wage for the first time in my life, so I put it to good use and went and saw a financial adviser', she said. 'He was amazing. I'd picked up his book when I'd hit rock bottom and read it cover to cover. The first meeting we had I was a wreck. I was seriously considering filing for bankruptcy and I was only 25. I think you should go and see him.'

'I'm willing to give him a go. I know it doesn't seem like it, but I really do want to sort myself out. I can't believe I went and bought the bloody plane ticket as though I didn't have a care in the world. I really think I'm beyond help.'

'I'll go and get Jason's number before you change your mind.'

Later, as I was walking down the hall to my bedroom, I saw a pile of mail on the hall table I hadn't noticed when I had come in from work. The letters included the usual suspects: phone bill, internet bill and a couple of other inconspicuous looking envelopes I thought must have been superannuation reports. I was so weary from talking to Eliza I put them on the floor next to my bed and fell asleep on top of the covers with the light on. I only woke up on time for work the next morning because Tom rang the doorbell.

After all the drama of telling Eliza I was in deep shit, it still took me a few days to get up the courage to phone Jason, the financial adviser. When I finally did ring I was promptly told by a stern-sounding receptionist that it would be at least three weeks before Jason's next available appointment, but I could put my name down on a waiting list to see him earlier. There must have been a hell of a lot of people in financial strife for this guy to be so busy, I thought.

Lessons learned

- Walk or take public transport to work – it'll help save you dollars and it's good for the waistline!

- It is possible to make sacrifices – instant coffee isn't the worst thing in the world.

- Reduce the number of nights out – revisit, or sign up to, your local video store. Just remember to return the DVDs on time …

- Take stock – reassess your expenditure and work out if there is anywhere else you can cut back.

- Suss out the best places for a cheap meal.

- Personal finance books can offer some great advice.

- Talk to your friends – find out their saving and get-out-of-debt strategies.

- Don't be afraid to ask for help. If you're not having any luck getting on top of your debt, consider seeing a financial adviser.

PART IV

The awakening

8 June to 9 August

Universal credit card: $1850 owing
LAND credit card: $850 owing
Wealth credit card: $3000
Parking fines: $400
Happiness: slowly growing

I woke up on 8 June, the morning of my first consultation with Jason, and was beside myself with anxiety. The night before I'd been awake until 3 am filling a manila folder with every piece of my financial history I could rustle up, in an attempt to look like the organised person I was aspiring to be. It may have seemed a little over the top, but I figured if I was going to see a financial adviser, it would be helpful to have the relevant paperwork on hand so he could see exactly where I stood.

'Those are all your statements?' Tom asked. He and Eliza had decided to stay at Eliza's the one night I actually needed some space.

'What do you think?' I snapped back.

Apart from being officially broke, I had also become the nasty person my ex-boyfriends had told me was lurking just under the surface of my sweet exterior. Tom and Eliza had counselled me for the best part of three weeks before the appointment, so there were no more secrets, and I was, again, indebted to my best friend for being such a rock. The possible results of the meeting were weighing heavily on my mind and as a result, the rules of friendship seemed to go out the window and I behaved like a complete bitch.

While I shuffled papers, Eliza and Tom had sat on the couch with a glass of wine each and watched me. I could have given a Monaco croupier a run for his money I was getting so good at it. I had avoided drinking any wine in case I inadvertently turned up hung-over and was pinned as an alcoholic, as well as a morally bankrupt saver who liked wine better then money. Of all the things in the world I wanted to calm me down before sleep, a nice glass of pinot was it, but I was determined to stay on the straight and narrow. I barely slept, and when the alarm went off I sat up feeling as though I had drunk three bottles of red. My mouth was dry and I'd had a strange night sweat that had left me freezing cold. Great start.

It wasn't Jason I was worried about; I knew he wasn't going to be a serious, old financial adviser with a budget stuck up his arse. What I was worried about was the utter shame of telling somebody I didn't know about the mess I had gotten myself into. I could only imagine what this pillar of the financial community would think of me: a 29-year-old woman with no dependants, no assets, no savings and massive debts. As I drove to The Firm's office a mantra started going around in my brain: '$5700 credit card debts, $500 rent, parking fines, no savings, no savings, no savings'. I was possessed.

Jason's offices were surprisingly chic, considering even I could afford to see him. The entrance to the two-storey 18th-century townhouse was white stone, with a chaise lounge strategically placed in a corner of the foyer next to an old oak coffee table. My lack of sleep made the idea of lounging overwhelmingly appealing, and when I sat down I nearly fell backwards, making the receptionist laugh—good start. Once she had stopped laughing she said Jason would be with me in a few minutes, so when a 30-something man walked out a huge oak door a second later I was still in the throes of trying to pull myself into an upright position.

'Maggie?' the man said. 'I'm Jason.'

Great, I thought, now I'm seriously looking sharp.

'Hi Jason, nice to meet you', I replied.

He walked me through to a conference room that looked over a pretty, ivy-draped courtyard and asked the receptionist to bring us some tea.

'Sit down and make yourself comfy', Jason said. 'You're looking a little bit worried. Are you okay?'

My money mantra had started going around in my head again, so when he spoke to me I jumped.

'No, I'm fine. I'm just looking forward to getting started', I lied.

'Okay, let's get down to business', he said. 'Why are you here today?'

I pulled myself together, took a deep breath and told Jason everything that had happened in the past six months. I explained that it felt like my debts were spiralling out of control and I was desperate to get on top of them, and I was scared I would end up a penniless elderly woman living off the pension. When I had finished he asked me what I was ultimately hoping to get out of seeing him.

'The bottom line is I want to clear my debts and have $10 000 in savings by the end of the year', I said, so matter of factly I didn't quite believe the words were coming out of my own mouth.

It felt like I was telling a psychiatrist my life story, but Jason wasn't scowling, he was smiling and nodding. When I started to explain again how I thought I was destined to be living in debt for the rest of my life he told me to stop.

'Okay, Maggie. You sound like you think you're in a pretty bad place', he said.

'You could say that.'

'Well, I can help you. Right now you're feeling like an idiot who has got herself into a whole lot of money problems and you can't see any way out. How many credit cards do you have?'

'Three', I said sheepishly—and, yes, I did feel like an idiot.

He didn't flinch.

'How much do you owe on each card?'

'Last time I checked I owed $3000 on one, about $2000 on another and about $800 on the third', I said. Saying the figures out loud made having three cards sound quite stupid. Why didn't I just have one massive bill?

'And how much interest are you paying on each card?' he asked

I told him I was paying 19 per cent on the Universal card, about 10 per cent on the LAND card and had recently applied for a third low-interest credit card to transfer the balance from my highest card so I could close it. He asked what had happened and I said the bank approved a new card but didn't tell me the amount I had requested to transfer was too large.

'They're bastards. That's how they get you', he said.

'I know. To tell you the truth I was surprised my application was even accepted.'

'So you have about $5800 in credit card debt. How much do you earn?'

'$772 a week.'

'Do you have any assets? A car or shares, maybe?'

When the word 'shares' came out of his mouth I couldn't stifle the laughter.

'Shares? God no. I do have a car, though.'

'What do you use the car for?'

'I need it for work in case I get called out to a job before I've left the house, and I've had it for so long it would only be worth a couple of thousand dollars.'

'How often do you get called out early?'

'Not that often, now that I think about it. I was driving it to work, but I've pretty much put a stop to that since it broke down and needed major repairs.'

I hadn't been called out early once that year.

'Getting rid of your debt isn't going to be a problem. You earn enough to get yourself out of this reasonably quickly and I'm going to hold your hand the whole way.'

Who was this man? I thought. He was so positive it was scary.

'I want you to come and see me again in a week or so with your last three statements on every account you have. When you leave today I want you to think about selling the car and anything else you have lying around you don't need. I want you to write a list of all your expenses and anything else you owe money on. You have to take responsibility for your debts; I can guide you but it is ultimately going to be up to you. What about your tax return? Have you done it?'

Another problem I hadn't seen arising. I had neglected to do my tax for two years. The first year I'd skipped it because of laziness and the next year I didn't do it because I thought the tax office was going to fine me for the year before.

'I haven't done it for two years, but I have all the relevant documents with me in this huge pile of papers.'

'Great. I want all your tax details too. You have a lot of homework to do, but I can't stress to you enough that it's all going to be okay.'

'I'm up for anything but I really don't share your optimism. I have terrible habits that I never seem to be able to break', I said.

'Like what?' Jason asked.

'I've tried to quit smoking for years, but when I get tipsy a cigarette is the first thing I reach for; I seem to have an insatiable appetite and no matter how much I worry about my weight the scales keep telling me I'm getting bigger; and, finally, I have never, in my entire life, been in control of my money.'

'Everyone gets pissed and has a sneaky cigarette and I don't mean to get too personal but you look pretty good to me. When it comes to the money, you have to understand, I see clients exactly like you every day. In fact, I met with one of my greatest success stories this morning and she was not too dissimilar to you.'

'Was she bankrupt?'

'No, but she was teetering on the edge. She had ignored any responsibility when it came to her finances and by the time she came to see me she was severely depressed and on the brink of a breakdown.'

'What did she do?' I asked, fascinated.

'Pretty much what I'm telling you to do now. We went through everything she owed and owned, and worked out a plan. Unlike you, though, she had close to $30 000 in debt and earned about $45 000 a year.'

'How long did it take her to sort herself out?'

'She was debt free in two years.'

'Wow, that's really impressive.' It really was. What the hell was I worried about?

'I've found that most people can be helped, but there has to be a commitment to the cause. With this other client, I told her to ring every single creditor she owed money to, explain her situation and see if a payment plan could be reached. Then we worked out a budget and went from there. I'm not saying it was easy, it was a very bumpy road initially, but we got there in the end and she's a different person — financially speaking.'

I walked out of Jason's office and I honestly felt happier and lighter than I had in years. In less than an hour he had reassured me my financial state was nowhere near as bad as I, or my friends, believed. In my jubilation I called everyone: Mum, who I got the feeling was shocked because I had not mentioned any of my drama to her; Eliza, who didn't sound surprised at all; and Max, just to gloat.

'You're doing it, Maggie', Max said.

'What?'

'You're fulfilling your Saturn Return.'

'Yeah, yeah, whatever.' I hated when he was right.

Sadly, it didn't take long for my doubts to kick back in. By the time I got home I had convinced myself Jason was mad and there was no way I was ever going to be able to get myself out of debt. I was sure there were things I had forgotten to tell him, things that would make him realise I was a hopeless case.

As soon as I opened the front door I headed straight to my bedroom to go back to bed. I was suddenly more tired than I had ever felt in years. I lent over to grab my novel and noticed a pile of white envelopes gathering dust on the floor. I couldn't put my finger on it but something told me the letters were a little too important to leave untouched beside the bed in the middle of a dust pile. As I tore open the first envelope my breathing quickened. I knew what this letter was, or at least I thought I did.

'Damn parking fines!' I shouted.

Despite the best of intentions, I had continued to avoid paying the parking fines and late fees I had accumulated, which had grown to more than $400. Now the local councils were coming for me with a court order. I either had to pay or get myself a lawyer and, unlike the video store fines, there was no way I was going to involve Eliza. I was just grateful she and my mum weren't in the room with me to see the letters. I couldn't have handled their knowing expressions.

My bad relationship with the parking inspectors of various councils started in my first year of university. I was constantly running late and the lack of decent parking around my inner-city university meant I often ended up leaving my car in weird and wonderful places in order to turn up to the compulsory tutorials. I was still living with my folks and when the late letters came I would act as though they didn't exist. However, my mother did and, like the kind-hearted woman that she is, would always pay them and leave the letters opened on my pillow like a maid would leave a chocolate at a hotel. But like a good holiday, Mum's generosity towards her only daughter did not go on forever and I was eventually forced to pay my own fines.

My appalling track record and spiralling debt hadn't stopped me from conveniently forgetting to pay the latest batch. The most recent letter said if I did not pay within a week of the letter being posted, I would receive another letter telling me I would have to go to court. As the first letter had ended up under my bed some weeks earlier, I wasn't surprised when I went through the pile of letters on the hallway table to find another letter telling me there was already a tentative court date booked if I did not pay immediately. They weren't even recent fines. On the back of the letter was a list of my misdemeanours and a few were backdated two years.

I was not going to let this go on any longer. I had promised myself I wouldn't use any of my credit cards until I was in Malaysia at Max and Jem's wedding, so I picked up the phone and paid the parking fines off in one hit with cash from my savings account. It was getting close to payday and when I checked my savings account balance after paying the fines, incredibly I had a few hundred dollars left from my last pay cheque — a miracle. Just to make sure I had killed off all the buggers I ran out to my car and checked on the dash and under the seat for any others. There were none — another miracle.

I had taken a day off work to meet with Jason and the next day I was given the third degree by Janice.

'Were you sick, Maggie?'

I decided to tell her the truth.

'No, I took an annual leave day to see my accountant.' That would shut her up, I thought.

'That should be done in your own time', Janice said, once again trying to assert authority over me.

What the hell was wrong with this woman? As I headed over to my desk I could see Spencer typing away. If I was with Spencer like Janice was, I would never be mean to anyone, I thought. And just as quickly as the Spencer thought had popped into my head, common sense prevailed and I nipped him from my mind.

It had been weeks and weeks since I had last tried to contact Margaret Black, so I was very surprised to hear a message from her on my work phone. She apologised for not returning any of my phone calls, but it seemed she had a proposition for me. One that she thought would be impossible to resist. I immediately picked up my phone and returned her call.

'My sister-in-law tells me she has a stalker from *The City*. It wouldn't be you would it, Maggie?' Margaret said sarcastically.

'I wouldn't say I was a stalker, per se. I just wanted to have a chat with her about Jack's antics and I thought, seeing he has openly run off with another woman, she would be more than keen to have her side of the story on the record', I said, trying to backtrack the awful truth of what I had actually been up to.

'She doesn't work that way. She's very hurt and she said seeing you parked outside her building and following her on her walks was like salt being rubbed into an open wound.'

I really had thought I had got away with following her on the walks without her noticing me. She must have thought I was a nutcase and a horrible person for not thinking that maybe she actually loved her shit of a husband for anything more than his millions.

'I didn't mean to upset her and, anyway, I've stopped the stake-out. What would you like to offer me? By the way, I thought you said you hadn't spoken to your brother in years? When did you get so friendly with his wife?'

'You never asked about her, so there was no reason to start shaming her good name to that rag you work for.'

Margaret seemed to have changed her tune since the last time I had spoken to her and it unnerved me. If it was such a rag, why was she even talking to me, I thought.

'Mrs Black, I'm sorry if I've upset you, or your sister-in-law for that matter, but I'm only doing my job and for the past few months it has involved gathering information on your brother. So far the only thing I have come up with is that he has left his wife for a woman who used to be married to his oldest friend. No-one will talk to me and to tell you the truth I'm starting to get bored to death of the whole saga.' It felt good to get all the stresses of the story off my chest.

'Well, that is bad luck.'

'What is?'

'They want to talk.'

'Who?' I said as my heart started to race. Had I spoken too soon?

'Kate O'Brien and Jerry James.'

I had. Jack's wife and his mistress' husband—a stellar journalism career suddenly flashed before my eyes.

'I think you might have just resparked my interest', I said, hoping she would ignore my comment about the story boring me.

'There is only one condition: you cannot bring a photographer when you meet them.'

'I'm sure that will be fine.'

I didn't know if it was going to be okay at all. The editor was going to want photos and I was going to have to tell Janice, as my immediate superior. There was no way I was going to get away with disappearing from work for a few hours without letting her know exactly what I was up to. When Margaret and I had organised a time to rendezvous a week later, I hung up the phone and stood up to walk over to Spencer's desk to share the exciting news, but something stopped me. I'm going to keep this one to myself I decided. I didn't want Spencer finding out about the meeting and taking control of the interview with Kate.

Since Spencer had turned up at the O'Brien stake-out I had gone out of my way to strike him from the record, so to speak. A pretty formidable task considering we sat a few metres away from one another in the same office. He sent me regular emails keeping me up to date on his investigations and I replied like a true professional. I still could not work out his motive for his visit and I was a little embarrassed I had developed a crush on him to begin with. Besides, the thought of liking someone at work was completely clichéd and I just didn't want to go there, no matter how handsome and seemingly sweet the person was.

That night, as Jason suggested, I pulled together the last three statements from my three credit cards and my savings account. I also wrote a list of all my expenses for our next meeting. I knew I'd turned a corner even if I still had my doubts. The week after the meeting I did everything right: I walked to work, made breakfast, lunch and dinner, and basically had a quiet week in, trying to spend as little money as humanely possible.

As part of my living thin program I had stopped going out for post-work drinks. This was as much to avoid Janice and Spencer as to save cash. But Genevieve decided it had been 'waaay' too long between drinks and asked me to meet her after work.

'I can't, Genevieve. I'm really trying to save money and I don't trust myself.'

'You can't stop going out altogether and, besides, there are things to discuss.'

'I haven't stopped going out, I'm merely exercising some restraint. What do you have to tell me that we can't discuss right here in the office?'

'I won't tell you unless you meet me for one drink.'

'Bloody hell, Genevieve. How old are you? It's not going to happen.'

I really was becoming a bitch. I had never spoken to Genevieve so sharply. Fortunately, she didn't seem to notice.

'How about tomorrow night then? You haven't been for a drink on a Friday night in what seems like months.'

'That's because the last time I did I was confronted by Dave and a huge bill. This might surprise you, but they both put me off doing any work-related socialising.'

'All water under the bridge.'

I had lost interest in fighting her. Also, I did have the O'Brien interview on Friday and would probably need a wind-down drink by the evening.

'Fine, I'll meet you tomorrow, but I can't have a big night. I'm really trying to get my act together.'

'Brilliant. I can't wait to see your face when I tell you what I know.'

Genevieve must have had something very juicy to pass along. I had never seen her so excited.

On Friday morning I arrived at work at 7 and immediately approached Janice to reveal that I was off to speak to Margaret Black, Kate O'Brien and Jerry James.

'Good work, Maggie. You're finally making headway. What's the plan?'

I was in shock. She had actually praised me.

'Obviously I want Mrs O'Brien to talk about her husband's affair, but I also want her to give me some background information on their life that no-one else knows and find out whether she thinks her husband was lucky to be released from jail.'

'You're going to have to tread very carefully. If you scare her off, then we may never have contact again. You do realise this will be the first time a journalist has interviewed her since her husband was arrested? I think you should take Spencer with you, as well as a snapper.'

I just couldn't get away from that man—Janice was probably making sure that I didn't scoop the story out from under his good-looking nose!

'She said no photographer.'

'Okay then, just take Spencer. If you can convince her to be in a quick picture, take a photo with your phone. It worked well when you caught her husband at the airport. Don't stuff this up, Maggie. It's a big break for you.'

I was fully aware of the delicacy of the situation at hand and didn't want to share the glory if I got the story, especially with Spencer. However, it seemed I had no choice because before I knew it Janice had called him over and was giving him the lowdown on my scoop.

As we drove to Margaret's house Spencer couldn't contain his excitement.

'Well done. There's so much Kate O'Brien can tell us. I've tried to get her to talk for years and she hasn't budged. You must have made a great impression on Margaret for her to have talked her sister-in-law into speaking to you, but there's no surprises there.'

'Thanks.' I was blushing again. This man had a very strange effect on me; I was either angry or acting like a dithering fool. I tried to ignore the smidgen of flirting and focus on the task ahead.

'How should I approach her?' I asked

'I guess you'll have to feel out the lay of the land when we arrive. You should probably tell Margaret I'm coming along.'

I called Margaret and she sounded a little put out that I was bringing someone along, but I reassured her that it wasn't a photographer.

Spencer and I spent the rest of the hour-long trip discussing the possibility of Kate telling us anything we could use for the paper. We decided because she had wanted to meet with me it was probably best just to let her talk.

'As I said, let's just assess the situation before jumping down her throat', Spencer advised.

When we finally pulled into Margaret's driveway and could see the blue water of the bay behind her house, I got incredibly nervous.

'What if I stuff it up?' I asked anxiously.

'You won't, Maggie. You're a great journalist and a lovely person. It will be fine.'

With Spencer's kind words still swimming around my head, we got out of the car and walked to the front door.

'Come in Maggie and Mr …?' Margaret said when we knocked on the door.

'Mrs Black, this is Spencer Lee. He's been working with me on the story.'

'Nice to meet you, Mrs Black', Spencer said.

'I know your work, Spencer', Margaret said. 'You were the first journalist to cotton on to the fact my brother was up to something. Come in.'

As we walked through her beautiful home I could hear a woman's voice talking in one of the rooms we passed.

'Let's just give Kate a moment to get off the phone', Margaret said.

Margaret led us into her kitchen and told us to sit down at her huge marble kitchen table, which was laid out with a white Villeroy & Boch coffee set — something I had had my eye on before I started living thin.

'Unfortunately, Jerry wasn't able to make it today, something came up.'

'Oh, okay', I said. I was a little disappointed he wasn't going to be there because I thought he would have made Kate feel more relaxed. And he would have given us an insider's perspective on O'Brien's business affairs.

When Kate finally got off the phone and came into the kitchen I hardly recognised her. Gone was her exercise gear and in its place were stunning black silk pants and a crisp white shirt.

'Kate, this is Maggie Rose and Spencer Lee from *The City*', Margaret said.

'Hi Maggie, nice to see you again', Kate said pointedly.

'Nice to meet you, Mrs O'Brien', Spencer and I chorused.

'Call me Kate', she said. 'Let's get down to business. 'I want to set the record straight. There has been a lot of misinformation printed in the press and, for the sake of my children, I want to clear everything up. Yes, my soon-to-be-ex-husband is a scoundrel. Yes, without any one of us knowing, he set up his Ponzi scheme and stole millions. But you both know that. What I want to do now is ruin him once and for all. Seeing him plastered across *The City*'s front page with his latest mistress was the final straw.'

Wow, this woman knows what she wants, I thought. I liked her instantly.

'What is it you want to set straight?' I asked.

'As far as everyone else is concerned, he went to jail and has walked out a free man, cleared of his crime. I was as surprised as anyone when he won his appeal and there is nothing we can do about that now. What we can do something about is the millions he transferred into a Swiss bank account after ripping off Shamrock Enterprises.'

'But he left Shamrock more than 20 years ago', Spencer said, pulling up his chair excitedly.

'I'm fully aware of that. Jack and I had just married when he took over at the helm of Shamrock. The Shareef family was wonderful to us. They bought us a penthouse in Dubai and treated us as though we were part of the family. It was an incredible time for both of us.'

'So what went wrong?' I asked.

'We had been there for about a year when I started to notice Jack had changed. As the chief financial officer he was in control of millions of dollars in investments and business deals on a daily basis. He had finally reached the big time and I could see he wanted it all for himself. There was absolutely no room for error and the stress was eating away at him', she said before stopping to light a cigarette.

'When Jack and I met I was deeply attracted to his strong will and charisma. This was a man who knew where he was going in life. Initially, the only thing I noticed that was wrong was that he had shunned his family. Margaret was the only member he invited to our wedding and no matter how many times I tried to probe, he didn't want to talk about them. He just said he had moved on. Our life in Dubai was opulent, to say the least, but I was miserable. When I noticed the stress starting to seep into our marriage I turned to Margaret for advice.'

'Jack always dreamed of living the high life', Margaret broke in. 'He was brilliant at school and university, and always seemed to have a number of business deals on the go. He just never seemed to be able to hold onto the money—not a fortnight would go buy before he would ask Dad or I for a loan. He was like a rollercoaster: when he was flush with cash he would be in great spirits and would be out to all hours partying. When he had spent it all he would fall into a deep depression.'

Although I was transfixed by the story I was starting to feel deeply disturbed by the similarities between Jack's and my own relationship with money.

'When he went away to study in London I thought he would put it all behind him, but all that changed was that Jack went from being a rock-solid member of the O'Brien clan to barely remembering to call at Christmas. He was embarrassed by us, or at least by our lack of mega wealth', Margaret said before standing up and putting on another pot of coffee.

Kate went on to tell us that their life in Dubai came to an abrupt end after Jack botched a massive deal with a Saudi Arabian oil company. The head of the Shareef family had asked Jack to buy a 45 per cent stake in the company, which would have made Shamrock Enterprises billions. But Jack didn't seal the deal and the next week the O'Briens left the country.

Despite Jack being out of a job, they had more money than Kate had ever dreamed. She knew something wasn't right, but when she asked her husband he dismissed her concerns and said he had been paid a bonus when he left and was going to start out on his own.

'I would never have dreamed that Jack had ripped off the Shareefs. I started doing my own investigating and found details of a bank account in Switzerland. There had been five transfers made, totalling $20 million, from a Saudi Arabian bank. At the time I didn't put two and two together, but when he was arrested it was one of the first things that crossed my mind, making me doubt my husband's protestations of innocence', Kate said before lighting another cigarette and pouring herself a coffee.

'So where do we come into all of this?' I asked when she had finished talking.

'I want you to expose him for what he really is, and the best way to do that is to shame him across the front of a newspaper. Since you put so much time and effort into following me, I thought it was only fair I give you the story.'

I said we would love to help and organised a tentative date to meet again, by which time Kate should have pulled all the relevant documents together.

'Are you sure it isn't easier to do this at your place?' Spencer asked Kate.

'No. I don't want anyone knowing what I'm up to. Jack is away for another few weeks, so I'll bring the papers I have stashed at home and we can start from there.'

'Before we go, Mrs O'Brien, is there any chance you'll go on the record and comment on your husband jetting off with Haylee James?'

I knew I was pushing my luck, but I had to ask so I could hold my head up when we got back to the office. I already had the scoop of the year in the palm of my hand, but Janice was a pit bull and I thought she would want something straightaway.

'I won't go on the record just yet, but you can tell whoever it is you report to that what I have to say will be worth waiting for', she replied.

'Can you believe that just happened?' Spencer said as soon as we were back on the road. 'If what Kate is telling us is true, this could be huge.'

I called Janice and filled her in on what had taken place. She was as excited as Spencer and me, and told us to take the afternoon off. I was in shock again. What had happened that had made the woman go from being a complete bitch to treating me like a normal human?

'Let's celebrate', Spencer said, as soon as I had relayed we didn't have to get back to the office.

'Um, okay', I said before I remembered that I had agreed to meet Genevieve.

She was a pretty easygoing friend so I didn't think she'd mind too much. I knew she had something to tell me, but I suspected it was a bit of office gossip. I sent her a message hoping it would suffice until the next day.

We dropped the car back at work and walked across town to a little wine bar. At first we talked about Kate's story and every possible scenario that was ahead of us, but by the third glass of wine we had started talking about ourselves and what we both wanted for the future.

'You're destined to be a star, Maggie Rose', Spencer said smiling.

'You're full of crap', I said. 'How would you know what I'm destined for?'

At that moment Genevieve called me. The woman had impeccable timing.

'Hi, Genevieve. What's up?'

'Are you still with Spencer?'

'Yes, why?'

'I'll be quick: he's not with Janice, he never was. Go get him tiger.'

I laughed and hung up the phone. As soon as I looked back at Spencer, the mood had changed to something far more interesting. We kept talking but now we were finding ways to flirt. After months of trying to pretend I wasn't interested in him, I could feel emotion flooding my chest and I realised just how much this man meant to me. Spencer kept brushing imaginary hair off my face and I could not stop myself from touching his arm as we talked.

At about 10 pm he told me his roommate was having a party and asked if I wanted to go along. I said yes, and as I went to get some cash out of my wallet he stopped me and paid the bill himself. Loved it.

We caught a taxi and I got in the backseat, half expecting Spencer to sit next to the driver, but he got in beside me. As I fastened my seatbelt I felt his hand take my chin. He turned my face towards him and kissed me. As we kissed he pulled me closer to him and wrapped his arms around my waist. I was in heaven. He smelt good and felt good.

'Finally', he said as I pulled my face away.

When I looked up I could see the taxi driver giving us a dirty look in the rear vision mirror. I didn't care. My tummy was fluttering with anticipation and all I wanted to do was get Spencer home. When the taxi pulled up at his house, he jokingly asked me in for a coffee.

'Coffee my arse', the driver said as we got out of the car.

Spencer lived in an old warehouse he shared with his friend Nathan. As soon as we got to the front door it was clear there was a party going on. There were about 20 people inside and the Rolling Stones were blaring from a vintage record player in the corner. Spencer led me into the kitchen to find Nathan.

'The famous Maggie Rose', Nathan said taking my hand. 'I was wondering when I would finally meet you.'

Spencer handed me a drink and we went into the living room to sit down and talk to some of his other friends. It seemed they all had heard about me. While we were sitting there canoodling I asked him why he hadn't asked me out before.

'I was going to ask you out the night Dave made a fool of himself, but you seemed to make it very clear you weren't interested.'

And that was that. My utter stupidity and stubbornness had not only ruined my finances, but almost a shot at romance as well.

It was an incredible night. We sat up talking and drinking until about 4 am before we fell into bed and promptly passed out. I woke up the next morning, fully dressed and deliriously happy. I could smell the wine coming from my pores, but I didn't care.

When Spencer woke up he rolled over and gave me a quick snuggle before going to make us coffee. I walked downstairs to his living room to find my phone and I had eight missed calls from Genevieve. I quickly called and gave her the lowdown, and then ran to the bathroom to make myself presentable.

While the coffee brewed I helped Spencer clean the kitchen, and we arranged to go out the next week. When I told him I had to get going, he walked me to the front door, opened it, then it shut again and pushed me against the wall and kissed me.

I did the walk of shame home in my work clothes and thought about all the men in my life I had met before Spencer. I didn't want to jump ahead of myself, I just felt as though he was the only real man I had truly met in my whole life and I wanted him.

I spent the rest of the weekend doing an inventory of my belongings and piecing together my shattered finances for my next meeting with Jason. I drove over to my parents' place and assessed what I had stored in their garage. There were a few things that could possibly go on eBay, but I wasn't quite desperate enough to sell off my only worldly possessions just yet.

As far as the car was concerned, I didn't know if I had the guts to sell it. I had bought it second-hand a decade earlier when it was only five years old. The previous owner had come into his own money problems and was forced to sell the car back to the dealer. Sentimentality was probably not the best reason to hold onto a car, but I had to figure out if I could survive without it.

At my second meeting with Jason, on 17 June, he told me he had prepared a budget for me and that one of his colleagues would be doing my tax returns for the previous two years. I handed over a folder full of the statements he had asked for and prepared to talk business.

'As we stand, you have just over $1400 in the bank and no bills to pay for another fortnight. Far more money than you led me to believe you had in savings. Now, have you given any thought to selling your car?'

I explained that the savings figure was a new development and I had thought about selling the car but just wasn't sure I could part with it.

The truth was I hadn't used it much since it had been repaired. I'd got used to walking to work and I had actually started to lose some weight. The car was also on its last legs and if I was going to be serious, it really needed some heavy-duty work done to it or it would collapse in a heap.

'You don't need it, Maggie', Jason sternly told me, reading my mind.

'It's my main asset, though.'

'Let me put it to you this way: if you sell the car and get $3000, it will pay off the Wealth card in one go. This will mean you will be paying about $400 less interest per month. That can go directly into your savings.'

Damn it, this man was taking too much sense for a Monday afternoon.

'I'll keep thinking about it and get back to you. Isn't there anything else I can do?'

'If you want to get out of debt, this is the quickest way to make it happen. You should also have close to $3000 coming to you from your tax returns.'

'Pardon. Did you just say $3000?'

'What did you think you were going to get?'

'I hadn't thought about it at all.'

'We'll talk more about your tax return next time. There's one more thing I want you to do before I see you next. You have the $1400 in your savings account and you still owe $850 on your LAND card. I'd advise you to pay off the LAND card and close the account.'

'I can do that.'

Once again I left Jason's office in high spirits. First cab off the rank was to pay off the LAND card and I intended to do it straightaway, like ripping off a band-aid. As I approached the shopping strip where the bank was located, the closest car park I could find was about 300 metres away. All I had to do was walk up to my savings account bank's ATM, withdraw the money, then walk next door and close the LAND account. As I walked the short distance up the hill I went into a clothing store to kill a bit more time. I was hysterically nervous. It was as though I was about to sign my life away or go on a first date. Would I have enough money to afford dinner with Spencer? I thought. I really needed to get my hair done. How much money would I have left over to pay for my groceries? Maybe I should just wait a week and pay it off when I had more money in my savings account?

A sudden rush of anger came over me and I was resigned to the task. I marched up the hill to the bank, took out $850 from the ATM outside and went inside LAND and closed the account.

You beauty, I said to myself as I walked back to the car. I did it. I had never been prouder of myself in my life. I had finally paid off a credit card with my own hard-earned cash and it felt incredible. As I walked back to the car I did a mental calculation of my week's wants and needs. I had $550 left: I needed to put aside $130 for next month's rent, $80 for food would be enough to see me through the next week, $50 for the blow-wave and $40 for dinner (providing we went somewhere cheap). I had $250 left over and for once I actually knew I could afford to treat myself! I stopped in a clothing store and as I perused the racks I spotted a pair of stunning snake-skin flats. Before I knew it I was handing over my savings card to pay for them. They were only $100 so I was still in the black.

I jumped in the car and drove home with a massive smile plastered across my face. I needed to celebrate. It was only Monday, but I didn't care. As soon as I unlocked the front door I called out to Eliza.

'I'm in the kitchen', she called back.

'I have an announcement to make', I said sitting at the kitchen counter.

'Does it involve Spencer or Jason?'

'Jason. I paid off one of my credit cards this afternoon.'

'That's fantastic! We need to celebrate.'

'I was thinking exactly the same thing.'

We opened a bottle of champagne Eliza had been given for her 30th and sat at the table chatting away as though I had just won the lottery.

'I was so scared, Eliza. I really didn't think I had it in me. My legs were as heavy as lead and I seem to have developed some heart problem where every time I get remotely excited or nervous the poor thing goes off like the clackers.'

'I know that feeling. What else did Jason say you had to do?' Eliza said, obviously as excited as I was about the progress I had made.

'He told me to sell my car, but I'm not so sure about that.'

'Do you need it?'

'Needing is not the problem. I've had a car since I was 18 and cannot imagine life without it. How would I get to Mum and Dad's?'

'Maggie, you go over there once every two weeks at the most. Surely public transport would suffice.'

'I'm just going to have to think about it a bit longer. On a more pressing note, I have a date with Spencer on Thursday night.'

'And?'

'I'm just excited, that's all.'

'I think at this point whether to sell the car is the more pressing problem. It sounds as though you have Spencer sorted.'

As always she was right. I had the man right where I wanted him.

Within a couple of days I had come around to the idea of selling the car. I hadn't driven it to work in ages and as a result I had no parking fines, no petrol to worry about and since the repairs it was in the best shape it was going to be in if I was going to sell. And I knew I didn't need it anymore.

On the down side: I had a close affection for the old Volvo. I had purchased it 10 years earlier, with the help of my parents, and it had never broken down or cost me much to run. I was going to miss the freedom of being able to take off whenever I wanted.

However, once I got my act together selling the car ended up being a far simpler process than I thought it was going to be. I rang John, the mechanic, and asked him for some advice. He said it would need about $4000 in repairs over the next few years and would probably only sell for that much — if I was lucky. My mind was made up — the car had to go.

John said I had a few options: I could either sell it privately, trade it in, or find someone who would buy it for cash as it was. Selling it privately required a full service and a roadworthy certificate, something I really was not able to afford at that time. I also couldn't afford to buy a new car, so trading it in was not an option either. That left finding someone to buy it just as it was.

After much online searching I found a company called Sell Pronto that quoted me over the phone without seeing the car and said if I agreed to their figure they would come and take the car away. The price range they gave was between $4000 and $5000. Although the car had been good to me, I had not always returned the favour. A badge was missing off the rear, it had a small dent in the front (from when it took on a life of its own one rainy morning and skidded into the tow bar of a car in front of me) and a few other bits and bobs that needed attention.

The man from Sell Pronto said there was no need to fix anything, but I wasn't taking any chances — I wanted that $5000. I decided I could afford to spend $200 sprucing it up, so I located a new badge, had it detailed and bought a new mat for the floor of the driver's seat. She scrubbed up pretty well and looked better than she had for about five years. Every evening for the next week I walked out to the street and admired my handiwork.

I made the most of the cleanliness and drove everywhere in the lead-up to the car being taken away. I even found myself stroking the dashboard and talking to the vehicle. I must have looked very strange sitting at the traffic lights tenderly running my hand across the black dash as though it were a long-lost lover. It had been a good car and it had taken me from A to B with only a handful of hiccups in the 10 years of ownership. Because of the dent, and the fact that I had got the year of the car wrong, the man who bought it said he would pay only $3800. It was less than I wanted, but as I was signing the paperwork I saw that my registration was due in a few weeks and that would have put me $600 out of pocket.

There was going to be no pussyfooting around when I walked into the Wealth Bank to close the credit card. I was all business. I was once again back on track on my mission to live thin and be debt free, and all of a sudden there was a light at the end of my financial rabbit hole. Within two days I had sold the car and paid off the $3000 debt on the Wealth card.

When I got home I emailed Jason to tell him the good news and he shot me an email straight back.

From: Jason Cunningham
Sent: Monday 22 June 12:16 PM
To: Maggie Rose
Subject: RE: car

Congratulations Maggie,

You are now well on your way to being debt free. I've had one of the guys in the office look over your tax and you're going to get about $3200 back. When you receive the cheque I want you to use the money to pay off your Universal card and the extra $1200 can go straight into a new high-interest savings account I am going to get you to set up. When can you come in to see me to sign your tax documents and discuss your budget? We should do it ASAP. I think this is going to be the part that you find hardest.

Jason

Jason Cunningham
Director
The Firm

Despite the ominous tone at the end of Jason's email, I was eager to set up another meeting.

From: Maggie Rose
Sent: Monday 22 June 12:30 PM
To: Jason Cunningham
Subject: RE: RE: car

I'll call your receptionist and make a time to come in. I feel AMAZING. Now I just have to keep on the straight and narrow until next week.

Empowerment and money had always been mutually exclusive in my book, but they were now very much together at the forefront of my mind. I found myself setting little money goals to achieve each day. It didn't matter how small the steps were, every cent I didn't spend was heading towards the $10000. Almost as though I was wearing a pedometer and trying to walk it—every step counted.

In the kitchen each morning while I ate my breakfast I started to think about the amount of money I was saving by eating toast and drinking a cup of tea at home compared with grabbing the $10 toast and latte at the office. I was still making gourmet sandwiches for lunch and my taste for instant coffee, although waning slightly, was saving me about $30 a week. Previously I was on three cafe coffees a day, but I had changed that habit to allow myself one bought cup a day if I felt like it. To counteract the proper coffee cravings I also bought myself a bone china cup and saucer and a box of Lady Grey tea to drink at work.

The day before my first date with Spencer I was determined to make myself look good on the cheap. In the past I would have gone out and spent at least $200 on a new outfit and another $50 on a blow-wave. Although my hair had been dyed a month before and the colour was still holding, I wanted to look fabulous and a blow-dry could not be forfeited. In my mind there was something magical about the way a good blow-dry could make a girl feel. For the date with Spencer, instead of going up-market, I walked into a student salon near work and, for the first time in my life, had a trainee hairdresser do my hair. It cost $10 and, low and behold, I felt just as good as when I'd paid $50.

As far as the clothes went, once I actually delved into my closet and did some handwashing and sponged down a few other dresses I had a quite a selection to choose from. My mother would have been so excited I was actually wearing something I owned without going out and spending hundreds on a dress I would wear once and then banish to the back of the wardrobe because it harboured bad karma from a bad night out.

The day of the big date arrived and as much as I wanted to spend it at home preparing, I still had a full day of work ahead of me. When I locked the door as I left the house to walk to work I had no idea just how huge the day was going to be. I usually grabbed a copy of *The City* and its rival papers *Vox Pop* and *The Tome* to read when I got to my desk, but I felt so good about the way things were going I decided to relax and just look on the websites when I arrived at the office. It was the first bad move of that fateful Friday.

As was usually the case on the final day of the working week, the office was slow to get started and when I walked out of the lift, which opened directly onto the newsroom, I didn't notice anything different about the place, so I went straight to the kitchen to grab a coffee before I sat down to read the news at my computer. It wasn't until I looked up and noticed Janice sitting in the editor's office being ranted at that I realised something was up. The editor was never in before 10 am — it was just on 8 am — and I had never seen her even look at Janice the wrong way. Janice was the editor's trusty sidekick who was happy to play the hard taskmaster while the editor was busy putting out the paper.

It was more than an hour before Janice walked out, and as soon as I saw the office's glass door swing open I put my head down as low as it would go so she wouldn't notice me. Unfortunately, my plan fell considerably short as she walked straight over to my desk and threw down a copy of *Vox Pop* on my desk.

'What the hell is this?' Janice said to me though clenched teeth.

I looked at the page before me and it was a picture of Jack and Kate O'Brien looking loved up outside their local cafe. Jack O'Brien had not been seen since I had caught him leaving the country at the airport months earlier. As *The City* did not have the funds to send Spencer or I to chase him, it had simply been a matter of waiting around to see if and when he showed up on the radar and besides, we had his scorned wife on the record saying he would be away for another month, so I was more than shocked to see a picture of the pair relaxing at a riverside cafe.

'I have no idea, Janice.'

'Didn't you and Spencer tell me Kate had agreed to out her husband's dodgy business dealings and had agreed to another meeting?'

'I said that Kate told us her husband was an out-an-out crook and she wanted to bring him down.'

'You'd better find out what is going on pronto or you'll have some serious explaining to do.'

The first thing I did was call Spencer and warn him what was going on but when he answered the phone he sounded terrible.

'Shit, Maggie. That's not good. I'm sick as a dog, though, and there's just no way I can come into the office to help you out.'

'What about tonight?'

'I'm sorry, I think I'm going to have to cancel that too.'

My life was falling apart and it was only 9.15 am. I hadn't even had time to check my emails and that was when the third shock of the day came my way. As I scrolled down the computer screen deleting government press call after government press call from my inbox I noticed an email from one 'j.o'brien'. Why on earth was Jack O'Brien emailing me? This was not a good sign. I was too scared to open the message and it was only when

I looked up and saw Janice scowling in my direction that I got my act together and clicked on it.

From: Jack O'Brien
Sent: Thursday 25 June 11:11 PM
To: Maggie Rose
Cc: Jerry James
Subject: Confidential

Dear Ms Rose,

I have recently returned from a business trip to London with my assistant to find you have been paying a great deal of interest to my life. From sources, I trust as a journalist you will understand I can't reveal, I have been informed you have been staking out my apartment, scaring the living daylights out of my wife and meddling in my family affairs. This is as cordial as I am going to act on this matter. As you can see I have included my lawyer, Mr Jerry James, as one of the recipients of this email. If I find you have continued your futile investigation I will take legal action.

Regards,

Jack O'Brien
Director
O'Brien Affairs

Great, that was all I needed—a bloody legal threat from Jack O'Brien. I forwarded the email to Janice, and then picked up the phone to call Margaret Black and find out what her sister-in-law was up to. After all the crappy news I had received that morning I didn't think I could take another low blow, but I had to cover all my bases before Janice made her way to my desk, which was imminent if the scary stares were anything to go by.

Margaret was not in the least surprised to hear from me, saying she had been waiting for my call. Why the hell didn't she just call me, I thought. It seemed Kate hadn't done the dirty on me and she had a grand plan to screw her husband over once and for all. Kate, Margaret said, had realised after our meeting that the only way she was going to be able to keep track of her husband's wayward ways was to take him back into the family fold. He had been having affairs for years, so Kate said she knew this time would be no different and as soon as she called he would be on a plane home to make amends for his indescretions.

Margaret said Kate still wanted to meet with me but didn't know how long it would take before she was ready to talk. She just said there were plans underway and I would have to sit tight until then.

I was relieved to hear I hadn't been totally screwed over and was still in with a shot of getting a big break with the story. As I hung up the phone Janice made her way over to my desk and I told her the good news.

'You were lucky this time, Maggie. As I've said over and over, make this story work.'

Janice really was a psycho.

Spencer was sick all weekend, which meant there was no chance of a date. I was pretty disappointed and, coupled with the nasty email from Jack O'Brien, I was having a shocker of a week. At least my hair looked good. I didn't think Spencer had tried to get out of the date, but as confident as I tried to be, the thought definitely crossed my mind. If it weren't for the text messages he sent from his sick bed, I might have started behaving like a scorned woman—not a good look when you haven't even gone on a date yet.

When I logged onto my computer on Monday morning he had sent me a very sweet email asking me out again. I thought about playing hard to get for all of five seconds before I accepted. We arranged to have dinner on Tuesday night.

I got home from work the next day after spending all day covering a court hearing for a bungled real estate scam and had an hour to get ready. The blow-wave I had had the week before was well and truly washed out, and I didn't want to start getting my hair done every time I was asked on a date. Knowing my luck, he would cancel and once again I would be left with great hair and no-one to appreciate it.

Once I had showered I spent about 30 minutes in front of the mirror blow-waving the bejesus out of my locks and putting them in hot rollers. I still wasn't a pro at it and I promised myself if we made it to a second date I would pay the $10 again.

It was a warm evening so I put on a black strapless dress I had bought the year before, paired it with some calf-length Italian cowboy boots and I was ready to go. Spencer arrived on time and had a taxi waiting to whisk me across town to Allen's, a little bar on the other side of the city. Unlike our first night out together there was no shillyshalling; we were together. I had never felt as comfortable with another person in my life. It wasn't that we had a lot in common, we just gelled.

After dinner and drinks and a hell of a lot of innuendo, we hit the road. Nathan, Spencer's roommate, was away so it was back to his place again to see where the night would take us. Needless to say it ended well.

***

When I decided to start living thin to save, I was adamant there were things that absolutely could not be changed. When I re-read the list I had written in January, I could not believe how naive I had been about the reality of saving. Back then I was spending close to $300 a week on going out and the rest of the money went on clothes, taxis, food, books and hair appointments. Bills were paid at the last possible moment and my rent money was never put aside. My credit cards were running on a revolving door of cash going in and out, and I was too scared to even look at my bank balance when I was paid, for fear I would actually have to do something about the juvenile situation I had got myself into.

The next meeting I had with Jason, on 26 June, was all about my budget. First I signed my tax return so it could be sent off and I could pay off the Universal card. Jason then handed me the piece of paper with the budget printed on it and explained what I was up against.

When I sat down to study the figures I was shocked at the amount I had let slip through my fingers. Jason's budget said I had to pay myself first—that is, I had to put away $200 a week from each pay cheque into a savings account. On top of this I was to deposit an extra $135, which was the savings I would be making from not having to pay any interest on the three credit cards when I had paid off the final card in a few weeks' time. He said if I could afford to pay the interest, I could afford to save it.

What the hell had I been doing with my cash all these years? It was embarrassing to see how laissez-faire my approach to money had been.

Maggie Rose's annual budget

Maggie's income

	Weekly	Monthly	Annual
The City—salary	$1028	$4455	$53 460
Less tax and student loan repayment	$772	$3345	$40 140

Maggie's expenses

	Weekly	Monthly	Annual
Savings—pay yourself first	$200	$867	$10 404
Credit card savings	$135	$585	$7 020
Rent	$185	$802	$9 624
Health insurance	$7	$30	$360
Home insurance	$7	$30	$360
Mobile phone	$21	$91	$1 092
Internet	$7	$30	$360
Public transport	$10	$43	$516
Groceries	$100	$433	$5 196
Eating out	$50	$217	$2 604
Alcohol	$50	$217	$2 604
TOTAL	**$772**	**$3345**	**$40 140**
Surplus	**$0**	**$0**	**$0**

Every cent I earned was accounted for. It was going to be a stretch on my part, but if I stayed on the straight and narrow I would have $10000 in the bank by mid-January. By June I was expected to have saved a total of $22777—a pretty impressive figure that I honestly didn't believe I would ever achieve, and which would go a long way towards seeing me own my own home.

Jason said the first step towards my success as a saver meant I had to get up close and personal with the concept of paying myself first. This meant each week when I was paid, a certain amount was spirited away into another account before I had a chance to get my greedy hands on it. Just like I had done with my Universal card, except this time I would actually be making money.

My life had changed considerably since that fateful New Year's Day eight months earlier when I had been sitting in the steaming-hot work car outside O'Brien's penthouse trying to figure out where my money had gone. I did not doubt that I was still capable of spending up a storm, but I had a whole lot more faith in my ability to be responsible. Even so, I had never stuck to any kind of a budget in my life and Jason's budget only allowed $100 for frivolity, a figure I would have only previously stuck to if I had some strange animal flu and was incapable of leaving the house because of a draconian public health initiative.

The first month was tough because I had to stop and think every time I went to make a purchase. I didn't want to go to the supermarket once a week in case something came up and the food I had bought was left to rot. Instead I went shopping on Sunday nights to buy the essentials and fresh ingredients for at least two dinners and went shopping again on Wednesday to cater for the other meals. I had never been that organised in my life.

I used the money from the tax return to pay off my final card, and after more than six months of wrangling with my money I could finally see that I was on track to saving $10 000. I had cleared my debts and was putting $335 per week into a high-interest super saver account with 5.2 per cent interest earned each year. The only stipulation was that there was a $1000 minimum initial deposit—a natural high I had not felt since being picked for my high school swim team took over me when I was able to join.

As much as a miniscule part of me wanted to throw in the towel and return to the freedom of not caring where my money was going, I had moved on. Just like having a sober cigarette after only having smoked while tipsy, I knew a return to the days of spending on a whim was only going to make me feel like crap. And as much as I longed to give myself a trial rather than killing myself over any mistakes I made, I knew there was absolutely no wriggle room if I was going to get to $10 000.

Once I had paid the debts and had some cash in the bank I could see there were a few other parts of my life that could do with some tweaking. The eight months of living with Eliza and paying cheap-as-chips rent had done wonders for my mission. I knew it couldn't go on forever, so I decided to start paying her more than the $500 a month we had initially agreed on. Aside from the fact that she had been such a good friend, if I was really going to get my life in order I needed to start living in the real world and paying the rent I could truly afford. Together we decided an extra $300 a month would go straight onto her mortgage so that she could pay it off at a faster rate. This meant I had a serious responsibility to get the cash into her account on time as there was no way I was going to be responsible for her home loan defaulting.

There was one problem. After months of trying to get my bank balances under control, Jason's solution to my debts seemed way too easy. I mean, if all it took to clear the decks was to sell my car and do my tax return, I would have done it years ago. There was something he wasn't telling me—or I wasn't telling myself, come to think of it. Then it came to me—the next step to saving would only work if I took control and did it. It wasn't rocket science, but it was somewhat of a revelation for me!

For some reason I kept thinking about an article I had read in a newspaper's weekend lift-out years earlier. The writer was discussing the state of mind of people who had successfully changed their lives and with each person's experience there was an expert to justify the changes in the person's psyche that had given them the power to transform. The woman I remembered most was a 50-year-old mother of three who had been massively obese her entire adult life and after years of misery had finally decided to do something about her weight. What this woman did struck me—she told herself every day that she was going to lose weight and every day she told herself all the things she was going to change. Eventually, every positive thought along the way became a part of her everyday life. That was what I wanted to happen to me and somehow I didn't think my debt mantra was going to cut the mustard.

Lessons learned

- Meeting with a financial adviser can help ease your worries and put you on a path to getting out of debt.

- Don't put off paying any parking fines.

- Be ruthless when deciding what you can get rid of! Being sentimental won't get you out of debt.

- Paying off a credit card and closing the account is an amazing feeling!

- Going through your wardrobe instead of buying a new outfit can yield fantastic results.

- Having a goal and a realistic budget is essential to reducing your debt and building your savings.

PART V

Saturn Return

10 August to 12 January

Debt: $0
Savings: $4014
Happiness: actually happy!

It was 10 August. January was still a long way away and there were four major obstacles to contend with: Jem and Max's Malaysian wedding, my 30th birthday, Christmas and, of course, me—I was my own worst enemy.

The wedding was in early October and I knew the trip was going to be far less painful than it would have been six months earlier, at which time I probably would have applied for another high-interest card or a limit increase to see me through the week away. Jason also said he would talk to me about budgeting for the trip before I left.

My birthday was on 8 November. Despite my love of a party, celebrating my own birthday was not something I had ever been fond of and if the day came and went without so much as a card, I wouldn't have cared less. However, I knew my friends and they would expect me to pull something together for such a momentous occasion. I just had to find something to do that was simple, fun and didn't involve spending any money.

All I knew about the coming Christmas was that there was no way I was going to be in the same position I had been in the year before, when I maxed out a credit card at lightening speed and then was evicted shortly after. I just had to find a way to enjoy the festive season and give gifts on a budget.

Not having a car had made a huge difference—good and bad. On the one hand, I was much more organised, the walk to work had become one of my favourite parts of the day, I didn't have to contend with traffic, I had no petrol costs and I would never, ever get a parking fine again—well, at least until I got my next car. On the other hand, I really missed having the freedom of being able to decide I was going to head somewhere on a whim and there were some things I was just not able to do without having to catch four buses and a train when it used to take 10 minutes in the car, which was very frustrating. I also didn't think I would ever visit my parents again unless—God forbid—they came and picked me up as though I was 16 again.

Being on a strict budget meant I had to say no to about 50 per cent of my friends' invitations. This meant I was far more excited to see them all when we actually did catch up. It also changed the way we socialised in general. My weekly dumpling meal with Jem and Max turned into dinner at each other's houses every few weeks. Instead of dumplings, we took turns cooking dinner, and to save some more cash I started cooking meals for Spencer rather than offering to pay every second time we went out. This had the added bonus of having him at my home for the night without distraction. He also didn't complain when I cooked my tried-and-true tagliatelle with salmon and rocket for the fifth time in a row. It only cost $10 to put together and tasted incredible.

As my bank balance went up, so did my addiction to watching it grow. Every week, the day after I was paid, I logged onto the super saver website to look at the graph of my account. It wasn't easy living on a strict budget, but I was not prepared to make any more mistakes and my infatuation with watching my money grow kept me focused on the task at hand.

By mid August I still hadn't heard from Kate O'Brien and I was getting impatient. When I rang Margaret to find out what the hold-up was she told me I would have to wait because Kate had a lot going on. Well that was obvious. It didn't mean we couldn't have a five-minute conversation, though.

A month later there was still no word. I was in regular contact with Margaret and all she said was that I had to be patient. I thought about the O'Brien family a lot and wondered what had happened for Margaret to be happy to ruin her brother. When I finally plucked up the courage to ask her, she said she had lost all feeling for him many years earlier when their mother was dying and he didn't come to her deathbed or her funeral.

'Did he say why?' I asked, rather shocked.

'He said he was stuck in London in the middle of key business negotiations and there was no way he could come back.'

'No offence, Margaret, but you brother sounds like a piece of work. Why did Kate stay with him for so long?'

'You'd have to ask her that. From my perspective, I think part of her was in love with him and, as in most unhappy marriages, there were children to consider. They have finished school now, so she must think they are mature enough to take it all in their stride. They would know a lot more about their parents' relationship than anyone else.'

That night Spencer came over for another meal of pasta and instead of foreplay we discussed the O'Briens. I was sad for Margaret and I wanted to know what Spencer thought of Jack O'Brien's behaviour. I also needed to confide that I was losing hope of getting the story. It all seemed far too complicated.

'You should have heard the sadness in her voice—it broke my heart. Do you think Kate is going to give her husband away?' I asked.

'It's hard to tell. She was pretty upset when we met her and it may have been a kneejerk reaction to his cheating. It's also understandable that it could take her a while to get what she needs to expose him.'

'Margaret told me Kate has been in touch with that famous barrister Nigel Vernon. Apparently she's worried that if her assumptions about where Jack got the $20 million from when they were in Dubai are correct, she could be brought down as an accessory after the fact, or whatever they call it.'

'That's true. Maybe she doesn't want to go ahead with it after all. But enough about Jack and Kate, I want to talk about Maggie and Spencer.

'Really? What's so good about them?' I said cheekily.

'This', he said, as he grabbed my face and kissed me.

Neither of us had uttered a word about love, but there seemed to be an unspoken agreement that we were both going in the same direction. I had made so many mistakes rushing into love with the wrong men that I wanted to retain some semblance of mysteriousness before I fell completely into anything breakable with Spencer, and I was happy we were taking it slowly. So I was more than a little taken aback when two and half months down the track, sitting on my living-room floor, I thought he was about to tell me he loved me.

'I've had such a good time with you, Maggie. There's something I've wanted to talk about for a few weeks and being here with you now I think it's time to bite the bullet.'

I could almost see the 'I love you' on his lips. I wasn't ready. Things just didn't happen that easily for me.

'Please, don't. I need to take this really slow. I'm not ready to jump in headlong just yet, Spencer.'

'You don't even know what I was going to say. And when did I start putting any pressure on you. Why didn't you tell me you wanted to slow things down?'

I don't know how it happened but a huge fight erupted. It was almost as though we had both been bursting to tell each other everything we hated about one another except, well for me at least, not a bad thought had crossed my mind since the moment we got together. He said I was insecure and needed to grow up and start acting like an adult. I don't know why, but I said he was an arrogant arsehole who had his head firmly planted up his backside. Once the shouting stopped we sat silently opposite one another until he stood up to leave.

'I have an early start tomorrow', he said.

'Can't you stay the night?' I said, hoping I could salvage something from my stupidity.

'Not tonight, Maggie.'

I was an idiot. The loveliest man I had ever met hadn't said anything or done anything wrong and I was acting like a complete lunatic. He left a few minutes later and I fell into a heap on my bed. I loved him. I could feel it. What had I done?

After sitting up and thinking about my reaction until the early hours of the morning I came to the conclusion that I was jaded. My last relationship had cast so much doubt in my mind about my choice in men that I didn't have faith in any of them anymore. Even Spencer with his steely grey eyes, heartbreakingly gorgeous smile and kind nature hadn't been able to break through the barrier I had built around myself for protection. I needed to talk to him. As it was 3 am I thought it best to wait until a respectable hour.

Spencer had started sending me an email each day when he got into work, so when I arrived at the office the next day and my inbox was noticeably void of any Spencer messages, I knew I had stuffed things up. I could see his shoes sticking out from underneath his cubicle, but I didn't have the courage to walk over and say hello. I sent him an email instead.

From: Maggie Rose
Sent: Tuesday 16 September 8:55 AM
To: Spencer Lee
Subject:

Am I going to see you tonight?

He wasn't quick to respond and I sweated for 10 minutes before a message flashed on my screen.

From: Spencer Lee
Sent: Tuesday 16 September 9:06 AM
To: Maggie Rose
Subject: RE:

I need some time alone to think about what happened last night. I'm not happy with how it went. I think it's pretty obvious we are not on the same page.

Although I could feel my heart breaking, his response sent a surge of anger streaking through my body forcing me to fire back a feisty response.

From: Maggie Rose
Sent: Tuesday 16 September 9:09 AM
To: Spencer Lee
Subject: RE: RE:

I thought we needed to talk, but don't bother contacting me. I think we both know where we stand.

The words I wrote were intended to hit him right where it hurt. If he was going to break up with me, he should have just said it straight out rather than giving me the cold shoulder. I hated when people did that. It left you stranded in no-man's land until they decided it was time to talk. I wasn't going to put up with anything like that from him. I had wasted my time waiting around for my last boyfriend and it got me nowhere. I didn't know how I was going to go a whole day with him sitting only metres from my desk, though, so I told Janice I was going to find Kate O'Brien and instead took myself home to bed and cried.

At 6 pm I was jolted awake by my mobile phone ringing next to my head. I had slept the entire day. I grabbed the phone expecting to see Spencer's name on the screen, but it was Genevieve. I didn't particularly feel like going into the gory details of what had happened, but I knew she would be sympathetic.

'Are you okay? I saw you disappear this morning and you didn't look so good,' Genevieve asked.

'Spencer and I broke up in an email.'

'What happened?'

I told Genevieve about the fight and she said point blank that I was a fool. As if I didn't know that already. I had to talk to him. As soon as Genevieve hung up I rang Spencer. It went straight to his voicemail and I left a message asking him to call me. When he hadn't rung half an hour later I tried again, and again at 7.30 pm and again at 8 pm. Finally, my phone beeped and there was a text message from him once again telling me I needed to grow up and if that was how I spoke to someone important, he didn't think we were right for each other. How does one respond to a message like that?

I rang Genevieve and told her what had happened.

'It's really over. He said we weren't right together. I need a drink. Can you meet me somewhere?'

'Of course. I'll meet you at Monroe's in 30 minutes.'

As soon as I walked in the door of Monroe's I spotted Spencer sitting at the bar with Janice and Dave. I turned on my heel and walked straight out while dialling Genevieve's number.

'Of all the places and times to run into Spencer it was now. And he's with Janice and Dave.'

'It's okay, hon, I'll be there in two minutes. Just go to the place across the road.'

If Monroe's was the kind of bar you wanted to spend a quiet evening being consoled about a broken heart, the place across the road, which no-one knew the name of, was the complete opposite. It was a faux Texan ranch bar with tequila on tap and a mechanical bucking bull in the corner. I sat at the bar and ordered a beer and smoked the first cigarette I had had in months while I waited for Genevieve to arrive.

'This all seems very strange', Genevieve said after she had downed a shot of the terrible tequila.

'I know, but he was going to tell me he loved me and I completely freaked out. I just wasn't sure whether I was ready and now I know that I am I feel like a complete loser', I moaned.

'No, you idiot. I meant this bar is strange. I'm fully aware of your stupidity. I'm sorry to tell you this, but Spencer is a champion and you just look like the one that let him get away.'

'Thanks, you're making me feel so much better. And for the record, if you call me an idiot again I will thump you.'

'At this point it's better for me to be honest with you than to beat around the bush.'

'Please just be nice to me. It's been a really, really bad day.'

Two hours, $60, four rancid tequila shots, four beers and about 10 cigarettes later I had slightly broken my alcohol budget, but had enough Dutch courage to walk over the road and confront Spencer. Being the good friend that she was, Genevieve came with me, but walked far enough back to have a bird's eye view of the carnage to follow.

The confrontation didn't go as planned. Rather than storming into Monroe's and demanding Spencer explain himself, as I had envisioned, I only made it as far as the street where I tripped over the curb and was left with a gaping head wound. I didn't remember the fall; Genevieve had to inform me of the gory details a few hours later when I woke up in the emergency room of the busiest city hospital to find I had 12 stiches above my left eyebrow and a drip in my arm.

I had never been a patient in a hospital before and I was desperate to get out of there as soon as humanly possible. Aside from taking me to the emergency room, which I was going to be forever indebted to her for, Genevieve was not a lot of help. She kept falling asleep, leaving me to lie prostrate on the tiny trolley, listening to the bizarre chanting of the girl in the cubicle next door who had overdosed at a trance party. I was released at 6 am with a bottle of painkillers and strict instructions to get some sleep.

As to be expected I didn't show up for work the next day. I spent it lying on the couch watching bad TV and worrying about the state of my life. Sure, I finally had some money in the bank, but what good was that if I was going to behave like an idiot and drink myself stupid. I was embarrassed and ashamed. By the time I finally dragged myself off the couch and had a shower Eliza was home.

'What the hell happened to you?' she said as I emerged from the bathroom with a huge white sheath plastered across my head.

'Spencer and I broke up, so I went out and got a little drunk, which then led to me falling over and cracking my skull open.'

'What happened with Spencer?'

Eliza was pure gold. She was the only person I knew who could completely ignore a head wound. I told her I didn't really know what had happened.

'He said he wanted to talk about something. Of course, I thought he was going to say he loved me and I freaked out. Then we had a massive fight and broke up.'

'You have serious problems, woman.'

'Thanks, Eliza. That's exactly what I need to hear right now. I will not be spoken to as though I am a five year old.'

'Spencer's wonderful. What kind of a person manages to screw something up with someone as devoted to you as he was?'

'Calm down. I tried to make amends but he wouldn't speak to me', I said as tears started rolling down my cheeks.

It had been a nightmare of a year. I had two months left of my 20s and all I wanted to do was crawl into a ball and hibernate from the world. I had managed to sort out my money problems and no-one had said a word to me about how far I had come, but as soon as I got dumped I was jumped on. The only consolation was that I had less than two weeks left of work before heading to Max and Jem's wedding, and one more day to get through before the weekend.

When I returned to the office a day later my head was still killing me and every second person wanted a blow-by-blow run-down of how I ended up looking like the Bride of Frankenstein. Not only did I have the stitches, but I had also developed a black eye. Spencer was out of the office making the day fractionally easier to handle and for some reason Janice ignored the fact that I had disappeared from work two days earlier and had returned with a massive cut on my forehead. I thought I was going to get through the day scot-free when Dave emerged from the lift and headed straight towards me.

'Ms Rose. How are you feeling?'

'Fine, Dave. You?'

'You don't remember anything do you?'

'I have no idea what you're talking about.' I wasn't in the mood to have Dave give me a hard time.

'I was there when you stepped in a pothole and fell over the other night, as were Spencer and Janice. It was classic slapstick.'

All of a sudden every drop of blood in my body shot into my head and I felt like I was going to be sick. Dave went on to tell me the three of them just happened to be walking out of Monroe's when I fell over. He made me feel a little better by filling in the blanks of the accident, though. I was really worried I had passed out or something, at least I had just tripped. What had my life come to if I was happy because I hadn't passed out? I was never going to get drunk again.

'Well, thanks for helping me out', I said with all the sarcasm I could muster as tears began to well in my eyes.

'We did, well Spencer did. He hailed a taxi and took you to hospital.'

I wanted to die. Not only had Spencer seen me hit the ground, he had also looked after me. Why on earth had Genevieve not told me? I finished the story I was writing about a paramedics' strike that was set to take place the next day and left work half an hour early. I needed to lie down and take stock of my life. I didn't want to hear from anyone so I turned off my phone and climbed into bed.

For the next two weeks I pretty much did nothing but go to work and come home. My only time out was my walk to work — the solitude did wonders for my savings and I could feel myself getting fitter by the day. Spencer and I were doing our best to avoid one another and the only contact we had was when he sent me an email asking if I had heard from Kate O'Brien or Margaret Black. I hadn't. My desire to bring down Jack O'Brien had vanished and I was content with being part of the general news mill again. Of course, I didn't say that in the reply email. I just said I would let him know if I heard anything.

How we had gone from being a couple to plain old colleagues was beyond me. And even though I knew I had made a mistake, his cold shoulder approach to my attempts to make amends and the raging red scar on my forehead didn't exactly make me want to walk over to thank him for taking me to the hospital. It didn't stop me from stealing glances at him as he walked around the room, though.

There was only one small hiccup on my savings journey in that time. Grace had called and said she wanted to have dinner before she left for New York. I arrived late to the Chinatown restaurant and found her fighting back tears. She had been seeing a guy she'd met a few months earlier and he said he couldn't wait for her while she was in New York. I felt terrible for her and as I was feeling miserable about Spencer we had the biggest Chinese dumpling dinner I'd ever eaten without Max, drank wine and cried. That part was all well and good. It was when we came to pay that the hiccup happened: Grace had forgotten to bring her wallet and I was left with the bill. I didn't care, though. She was so sad I was happy to blow my budget for a good friend.

I caught up once more with Jason, at the end of September, who said I could afford a $1450 budget for my two weeks away, and that could come out of my savings and my annual leave pay.

'You should be proud of yourself. You've stuck to your budget and you've come so far. I believe in you — go and enjoy your holiday', Jason said as I left.

I was glad he was happy with my progress, but I think getting dumped may have had a huge effect on the amount of cash I'd been spending. I wasn't hungry, I had stopped going out altogether and the video store attendant was becoming my best friend. I wasn't confiding in him or anything, but he had great taste in TV shows and I became addicted to *Studio 60 on the Sunset Strip*—an awesome series about a fictional sketch-comedy show based in Los Angeles.

And after all that, as much as enjoying myself was what I wanted to do, I was worried I would undo all my good work and come back from Malaysia with five Chanel handbags and be back in the red.

The Monday before I left, 3 October, I was paid my usual wage plus my annual leave and holiday loading payments. My super saver account balance was $8700 and of that I only wanted to spend $1000 on my week away, so there was some money left over for the week I was at home. The money had to cover food, drinks, sightseeing, the wedding present and anything else that cropped up. As far as I was aware Malaysia was an inexpensive place to take a holiday, but we were staying at a five-star resort and I was worried it was going to cost me about $10 for every can of Diet Coke I ordered from the poolside bar.

On Tuesday I left work early and went back to the hospital to get my stitches taken out. The wound looked like it had healed nicely and the nurse who removed them said she didn't think it would leave a scar.

I then went out and bought myself a good-quality suitcase, which was marked down 50 per cent to $250 for an end-of-season stock clearance. Who knew suitcases had seasonal styles? Buying the suitcase wasn't in the budget, but I had the extra cash from my annual leave so I went for it.

My flight was booked for Saturday morning at 10. To prepare myself for the eight days away I had taken the Friday off work and the first thing I did was organise my finances. I sat down with my laptop and paid every bill for the next month. To make doubly sure I didn't stuff up my savings plan and go on a wild spree, I also paid two months' rent into Eliza's account. I wasn't going to take any chances.

Next was my mobile phone. The thought of spending a week without contact with the outside world sent shivers down my spine. I arranged international roaming and the assistant in Jakarta told me to be careful of my internet usage, as it was a costly service. I had no intention of using the web while I was away, I just wanted to know I could use the phone if I needed to. I then sorted through my wallet and took out everything except my savings card and hunted through my wardrobe for the in-case-of-emergencies Wealth credit card. When I went to the bank to exchange some cash I saved myself a little extra by purchasing traveller's cheques, in the hope of cutting out any need to go to a bank while I was away.

There would be no new dress for the big day. Even though I was one of Max and Jem's witnesses, I couldn't justify spending hundreds of dollars on a new outfit I would potentially wear only once. My walking around town since I had sold the car had resulted in a five-kilogram weight loss and I was able to fit into a gorgeous short, gold Collette Dinnigan number I had bought on a whim for a cousin's wedding 18 months earlier. It had cost $500 on sale and because I had put on weight I had only worn it once, so I was in no danger of anyone having seen it before. I paired it with some gold heels and I was ready to go.

Once Eliza and I had both finished packing, I made us some grilled fish and a salad and we sat down for the first dinner we had eaten together in several weeks. As I cut into the salmon Eliza cut straight to the chase.

'Have you heard from Spencer?'

'No, nothing. It's so weird. I'm not sure what happened, but I'm pretty sure I put the final nail in the coffin when I face-planted the asphalt in front of him and he had to take me to hospital.'

'Yep, that was probably the clincher.'

Eliza went on to tell me she had seen him at a party a week before, but hadn't said anything to me because she didn't want to upset me. A first for her.

'What did he say?'

'He said he didn't think you were ready for a serious relationship.'

'Oh God. I miss him so much, Eliza. And I am ready for a relationship. I just had a second of doubt about how fast things were going. For all I knew he could have told me he loved me and the next week he could have been running in the other direction. It has happened before you know.'

'I told him he had behaved like a right arsehole', Eliza said bluntly. God I loved this woman. She was the ultimate ball breaker. I wanted to be just like her when I grew up.

'You did? What did he say?'

'He said he didn't understand why you'd reacted so badly when he was just going to ask you to go away with him when you got back from Malaysia, because he had some annual leave up his sleeve.'

I might have said it a million times, but I was officially the biggest idiot I had even known. The size of the ego on me; I was ashamed of myself.

'I had no idea. Why didn't he tell me? He must have known I thought he was going to say something else. Thanks for talking to him, but he hasn't said a word to me. I just want to get to this resort and lie with my head in the sand for a week.'

'Don't worry, Maggie. I'm sure it will all work out in the end. Just give it some time.'

Despite Eliza's optimism, I wasn't so sure.

We went to bed exhausted at 10 pm. Tom was going to pick us up in a taxi en route to the airport the next morning at 7 and we both needed a good night's sleep. When there was a frantic knock at my door in the middle of the night, I thought I must have overslept and I jumped out of bed to head to the shower. I opened my door to find Spencer standing outside the room leaning on the doorframe.

'Spencer, what's going on? How did you get in here?' I said, trying to cover up my near-nakedness with the tiny towel I had grabbed in my semiconscious state.

I looked down the hallway towards the front door and could see a light peeking out from Eliza's room. She was a shocker.

'Eliza let me in. I need to speak to you before you go away.'

I could see he was a little drunk, but he looked so irresistibly handsome and dishevelled.

'Let me say something first', I said. 'I love you. I'm sorry I freaked out. I'm a madwoman at times. I wanted to fix things the next morning, but by then it was too late and you were well and truly mad at me.'

'I wasn't angry with you. I just hated the way you became so insecure. I mean, things were going so well. I didn't want to be with a person who was going to freak out when someone was just trying to be nice.'

'You're going to have to learn to ignore me sometimes. I don't always react in a normal way.'

'I love you, too. You have to start trusting me and telling me things that are going on in your head. I'm not out to hurt you, I want to be a part of your life.'

He loved me—whoo hoo! I knew it all along.

The next morning Spencer waved Tom, Eliza and I off as we left for the airport and told me he would pick me on my return. I was completely blissed out and couldn't wait to be with him again. Eliza told me she had sent Spencer a text message before she had gone to bed, telling him to get his act together and sort things out with me before I went away because she didn't want to spend a week away with me if I was going to be miserable. I thanked her profusely and she replied in her usual matter-of-fact manner.

'I can't be fixing things for you forever. Make it work this time.' She was starting to sound like Janice.

We arrived at Kuala Lumpur International Airport at about 4 pm local time and were faced with the kind of humidity one can only experience close to the equator. We then had to catch another flight to get to one of the remote Langkawi islands off the north-west coast of Malaysia, where the resort was situated and where the rest of our friends, who had flown in the night before, were waiting.

The five-star resort overlooked a crystal-blue bay and to the rear was dense rainforest with walking tracks leading to sky-blue lagoons. My room overlooked the water and as soon as I had checked in Tim and Fran were at my door to take me for a swim and a poolside cocktail. It had been nine long months since I had shared a home with them and our friendship had become almost non-existent as a result of our busy lives.

As we sipped our cocktails we debriefed about the year behind us. Fran wanted to know if I had saved any money and whether I had sorted things out with Spencer. She was still happily single and loving life outside the bureaucratic doors of politics. Tim told me he was going out with his boss, Yvette — no surprises there — and was a few months off having his new cafe ready for business. I was so happy to see them. Things had changed so much since that fateful January night when they confronted me in the kitchen. I proudly told them how much money I had saved, about Spencer, about Jason and how sorry I was for what had happened earlier in the year. By the time we had finished talking it was close to 9 pm and we had to get ready for dinner with Max, Jem, Eliza and Tom.

When I got back to my room I had a good look around. I'd booked the trip quite far in advance, so I had been given a great deal on one of the best beachside suites the hotel had to offer. My room not only had a balcony overlooking the ocean, but a massive king-size bed and a fridge filled with tropical fruit and a bottle of Bollinger. I grabbed my phone to send Spencer a text and saw that he had called. I phoned him straight back and we spent the 30 minutes I was getting ready talking nonstop about how much we wanted to be in the room together.

The wedding was on Monday afternoon. That morning I got up and went for a long swim before sitting down to breakfast with Max, Eliza and Tom. There was no bridal party, but as Max's oldest friend he had asked me to be a witness and Jem had asked her sister, Pearl, to be hers. Ever the protagonists, Eliza and Max got straight into me as soon as our breakfasts were served.

'How's the saving going, Maggie?' Max asked.

'Very well, but haven't you got better things to talk about on the morning of your wedding?'

'Ask her about Spencer and her scar', Eliza added through a mouthful of fruit.

'I just want to relax and eat. You two will have to find something else to talk about.'

And with that they shut up. It was a miracle. I was finally making ground with my friends too.

The happy couple said their vows in an old church at the rear of the island before we headed back to the resort and danced until five the next morning. It was the best wedding I had ever been to. Jem looked beautiful and Max couldn't wipe the smile off his face. To honour our old tradition, they even had dumplings on the menu.

The rest of the week was spent swimming, reading and walking in the rainforest. I had taken three books that had been sitting on my bookshelf for two years and read them all.

Despite worrying about the cost of the week away, when I checked my traveller's cheques the day before I headed home I had amazingly spent only $900, which included my meals, a blow-wave before the wedding, a manicure and pedicure and two beachside massages. I still hadn't bought Max and Jem a wedding present and decided to wait until they were back from their round-the-world honeymoon to give them a gift.

With no thought of my next phone bill, I ended up talking to Spencer every day I was away. I just couldn't get enough of him. Now that we knew where we stood, I felt so content and confident about the future I just wanted to get started. He met me at the airport the following Sunday night and whisked me home for a night in. I had taken another five days' leave as it was the first holiday I'd had all year, and Spencer took me down the coast to his family's holiday home where we did nothing but cook, play Scrabble, swim and canoodle.

***

I returned to work a new woman. I was refreshed, in love and the scar on my forehead had practically vanished. I had forgotten all about the O'Brien saga on my two weeks' away and was pleasantly surprised to hear Kate O'Brien's voice on my work voicemail saying it was time to meet up again. I called her back and we arranged to meet at Margaret Black's house the next day. It seemed a few weeks' away had fired me up again. I went and told Janice and she said this time I would have no choice but to take a photographer because I needed to get moving with the story.

Although we had been working on the story together for most of the year, I told Spencer I wanted to go alone and he said he would leave it in my capable hands. If Kate was going to take down her own husband, I felt that I had put in enough hard work to be the only name on the story.

The next morning I arrived at work just before 8, signed out a work car and headed to Margaret Black's house with one of the photographers, Sammy. I told Sammy I had no idea what to expect; for all I knew Kate O'Brien could have called the meeting to tell me the story was off. I sincerely hoped not.

We knocked on the Black's front door a little after 9 am. Margaret and Kate had set up shop, so to speak, on the dining-room table. Hundreds of papers were stacked neatly on one end and Kate sat with a laptop and an ashtray in front of her at the other end. Once we had exchanged pleasantries it was straight down to business.

'I'm going to give you what I have', said Kate. 'My legal advisers have told me I can give you the details of my husband's dealings with Shamrock and I will not be incriminated. The $20 million that was transferred into his account was a legitimate transaction, but I have been in contact with the Shareef family and there was another dodgy deal I was not aware of.

'The week after our last meeting I went through every bank account Jack and I had together and found I had access to all but one — the Swiss account into which the original $20 million was transferred. I went though his office and home computer and all I could come up with was a statement for the account from three years ago.'

The statement Kate handed me showed Jack had been regularly depositing large amounts of money into the account, including one $15 million hit. I was in the wrong business.

'I knew it wasn't enough, so I did two things. As Margaret informed you, I told Jack to come home and be with his family. He is a philanderer, but he is also a family man and one call from his long-suffering wife was enough to get him on a plane home.'

The second thing she did was to call the head of the Shareef family in Dubai to find out the real reason Jack had split with Shamrock so acrimoniously.

'Ali Shareef became head of Shamrock when his father died 10 years ago. Although Ali was only young when Jack and I were there, he knew every detail of what had happened. He said his father had given Jack carte blanche to buy shares in an oil company being set up in Saudi Arabia. However, instead of putting the money into Shamrock's venture, Jack told the Shareefs the deal had fallen through and used $10 million of their money to buy into the venture himself.'

'Why did they let him get away with it?'

'Because of me. I was pregnant with our first child and the Shareefs told Jack if he left the country and promised to never have anything to do with them again they would let him walk away.'

I didn't even know where to begin. It was a huge story and I wasn't sure I could do much with it unless I had some hard evidence from the Shareef family. Luckily Kate was prepared and handed over a signed statement from Ali Shareef. It wasn't the kind of story that was going to send Jack back to jail, but it was enough to poison his name for good. There was just one more thing I needed from Kate. I needed her to go on the record for a separate story and tell me about her husband's affairs.

'I don't know if you're still back together, but my boss wants to know what happened with Haylee James.'

'Haylee is just one of many women my husband has had liaisons with. I'm happy to go on the record as I have left him and have been staying here with Margaret for the past week. I never had any intention of taking him back for good, but when my daughter came home three weeks ago and found Jack and Haylee in our bed it was the final straw.'

'Why didn't Jerry James come forward to talk to us?'

'He still loves his wife and is hoping for a reconciliation. He's also strangely devoted to Jack and decided to stay on as his legal counsel.'

That explained Jack's email a few months earlier. Sammy the photographer had sat patiently through the entire meeting and went straight into work mode as soon as Kate had agreed to go on the record. He was a true professional and knew exactly what type of photos the editors would want. We left Margaret's home with the paperwork and a series of 20 shots of Kate around the property.

When we got back to the office I went straight over to Janice to tell her what had happened. Then for the second time in my career, the first being when I was hired, I was taken in to see the editor. She was excited to say the least and mentioned a promotion several times as she sang my praises. I didn't even know she knew who I was, so to say I was flattered by the attention would have been a gross understatement.

To spark readers' interest, the editor decided to run Kate's story on the front page the next day and the follow-up story would be the information she had given me about Jack and Shamrock. There was no way Jack O'Brien was going to see either story coming. It was great.

I was on a roll. The story practically wrote itself and when I finished Spencer, Genevieve and Janice took me out to celebrate. We went back to Candle, the infamous bar where I had received the $108 bill all those months earlier. There was not going to be any such bill this time around, with Genevieve and I grabbing a wine menu as soon as we had found a table.

The four of us sat and talked nonsense for hours. When Janice was on her third glass of champagne she asked Spencer to move and came and sat next to me.

'I'm so proud of you, Maggie', she said.

I was in shock. This woman was so two-faced I didn't know what was going to come out of her mouth next.

'No offence, Janice, but you haven't exactly been Miss Supportive.'

'I'm not known for my tact. I was trying to help you out. I work on a philosophy of tough love. I knew you needed to be pushed.'

If that's what she called 'pushed' I'd hate to see her be mean to someone.

When we got home I decided I trusted Spencer enough to tell him all about my money worries. If I was going to be with this man he had to know the good and the bad. I started from the beginning and left no detail out, even telling him about the massive bar bill and the disastrous balance transfer that had pushed me over the edge.

'I'm glad you told me', he said. 'Eliza had actually already said something, but I wanted to hear it from you. I'm not so great with money either by the way. I'm 33 years old and I'm still sharing a house with my best friend, too.'

We spent the rest of the night talking about what we each wanted for the future and to my great delight, it was the same thing—each other.

The day after the Shamrock story ran I was not in the least surprised to see Jack O'Brien's mug on all the breakfast news shows as he defended himself. For one brief moment I thought of all the families and businesses he had ruined and hoped it was a small comfort for them.

The week of my 30th birthday arrived and started in the most Maggie Rose fashion possible: my phone bill arrived and was $600. The week away in Malaysia might have cost me only $900, but somehow my phone calls to Spencer managed to almost beat it. I didn't want to delve into my savings, even though I knew that was what I was eventually going to have to do, so I just sat and looked at the bill for an hour trying to figure out what to do. I could feel myself falling apart. I was doing so well, how could I let something like this happen? Of course making 30-minute international phone calls was going to be expensive—what did I think I was doing?

I called the phone company to find out where I had gone so wrong and found myself talking to someone in a Jakarta call centre again.

'Ms Rose, our records say you were warned about international internet roaming charges', the man said.

'I didn't use the internet', I replied. 'I only made phone calls.'

'Your international phone calls came to $200 and you obviously didn't turn off the internet roaming function on your phone because you have been charged $200 for that. The remaining $200 was charged by your regular local service. It doesn't matter if you're not using the internet, it still roams and uploads data if it's turned on.'

I tried to tell the man I wasn't told to turn the internet roaming off and he said it was not the phone company's responsibility to tell me that vital piece of information. He said he could put me through to financial services to set up a payment plan or I could pay the whole amount in full. I didn't want the bill hanging around my neck like a sack of smelly onions, so I hung up and paid online.

My savings account balance was down from $8700 to $5800 after my week in Malaysia and the phone bill, and I was worried I would fall back into my old ways. I needed to get tough on myself, so I told my friends I wasn't going to celebrate my 30th because I had to save some cash.

My birthday fell on a Friday night and after a busy day the only thing I wanted to do was have a nice dinner at home with Spencer. I wasn't fussed about presents and told all my friends there wouldn't be a party, which no-one seemed concerned by. I just wanted the day to be over and done with so I could get on with the next chapter of my life. I was more than happy to see the back of my

20s, because as much as I had myriad fond memories of the decade, I was ready to move on.

To treat myself I went and got a cheap blow-wave on the way home from work. I walked in the front door and the house was cool and quiet. Exactly what I wanted. Spencer had taken me out for a sandwich at lunchtime and said he would be over at 8 pm to cook me dinner. I had a shower, got myself dolled up for a romantic dinner at home and sat back on the couch ready for the night ahead.

At 8.30 pm he still hadn't arrived and I was getting impatient. I might have said I didn't want anyone to make a big deal about my birthday, but being on time would have been nice. When I heard a knock on the door at 9 pm I was starving and cranky. I opened the door to find Spencer standing with a bouquet of roses and a bottle of expensive champagne, but no food.

'You look great. Let me put this in the fridge for later. I'm taking you out for dinner.'

He told me he was taking me to Alex's, a great seafood restaurant around the corner. We arrived and it looked packed. I wasn't in the mood for crowds and almost went to say something when I noticed a whole table stand up and start singing Happy Birthday. Spencer had organised a surprise party with Eliza, Tom, Genevieve, Tim, his girlfriend Yvette and Fran. I was truly shocked, but should have figured something was up after everyone acted so blasé when I said I didn't want to celebrate.

I had a ball. The food was divine and they all made a huge fuss. Eliza and Tom gave me a set of very cool Chanel earrings, and Fran, Tim and Yvette all pitched in to get me tickets to a world-renowned theatre company that was touring the following year.

As we sat and ate dessert Eliza stood up and tapped her fork against a champagne glass to get our attention. It was speech time.

'I know Maggie has Spencer now, but I am still her best and oldest friend, so until she is married I'm going to be doing the speeches. It has been a long year for Maggie Rose and one that none of us will ever forget. When she moved into my house in January she was a sad, sad soul none of us thought we were going to be able to help. All I could do was offer her a bed.'

I had started crying at this point, making Eliza impatient. We weren't in bloody court.

'All I want to say is that we love you and are so proud of everything you have achieved', she continued. 'We always knew you had it in you. Also, Max and Jem asked me to pass on two things to you.'

The first was a letter Max had emailed to Eliza.

Dear Maggie,

You made it to 30 and I was right — your Saturn Return did change everything. You had an incredible year of upheaval, and Jem and I want you to believe in yourself a bit more before your next Saturn Return in 30 years' time. To celebrate your successes we're giving you something we know you will love, but now need more than ever on your quest for security.

All our love,
Max and Jem xo

They had sent me a beautiful Moleskine financial diary for the year ahead. It was tan leather and had everything a saver could desire, right down to a detailed budget planner.

Spencer waited until we got home to give me his present — an amazing black and silver Sonia Rykiel bracelet. I loved it, and him, more than anything. It was never coming off.

After my birthday I started to get worried again that I wouldn't make the mid-January savings target Jason had set me. I had about two months until the end of the year. I had added the stipulated $335 weekly savings to my super saver account, but I was still hovering around $6000 and there were only eight weeks until my deadline. By my calculations if I was to go along putting in the $335 until the start of January I would have been $1000 short of my goal, and I still had Christmas to contend with. There were going to have to be cutbacks.

The next day I went to my parents' house for my birthday dinner and while I was in the back garden with my dad I noticed all my furniture still stored in the garage. I walked in and stood staring at the lovely things I had accumulated and, as much as I was attached to the Danish-designed bookshelf, the antique chair and the bed, the only thing with real sentimental value was the painting my grandmother had left me when she died. Everything else, I suddenly decided, could go.

I had bought some shoes on eBay a couple of years earlier so I knew the drill, sort of. I went back to my parents' house the following weekend and pulled the bookcase, the bed and the chair out into the light to take some photos. This was the only step in the whole process I was actually au fait with. Once that was done I went back to my place and logged onto the eBay account I still had from buying the shoes and followed the instructions for selling.

The first thing it told me to do was take a look at the site and compare my furniture with other pieces up for sale. Next I had to upload the pictures and then I had to give the three pieces a detailed title so buyers knew exactly what they were bidding for. I also said the pieces were pick-up only. I did not want to be sending furniture around the world.

There were hundreds of similar beds and the frames most like mine were being advertised at between $100 and $200, so I wasn't completely shocked when at the end of the first lacklustre auction the highest bid was $120. The bookshelf and the chair were another matter. I had paid about $200 for the bookcase at a second-hand store a few years earlier, but I knew it was worth a whole lot more. It was an original midcentury Danish piece and was a one-off. The designer wasn't immensely famous, I had simply taking a liking to it because it was glaringly retro and wood. I would be sad to see it go. I listed it for sale at $300.

After five days of the seven-day auction there were no bids and I was secretly glad because it meant I could keep it. I sat at my computer for the best part of the last two days of the auction waiting for any kind of movement. If I had to leave the room I made sure Eliza, Tom or Spencer were around to take my place until I returned. I was obsessed.

On the final day, with two minutes to go, someone bid. Then another person bid, then the first person bid again. It was eBay tennis and I was going to be the winner. A furious bidding war ensued and it eventually sold for $500. Probably less than it was worth, but still a fat profit without too much effort. I was very pleased with myself. When I sent the winner a note to give him the transaction details I congratulated Rich from Surrey Hills for having a keen eye. I'm not sure if sending personal notes was in line with eBay etiquette, but Rich didn't say anything.

The chair was a classic B&B Italia design replica, which I had paid $50 for in my first few months of working as a journalist. I was loath to part with it, just because it was so cool, but I had inkling it might be an eBay hit. And I was right. The auction was stagnant for close to a day and I was dismayed to think no-one was interested, then, just like the previous auction, on the final day at the last minute two foreign buyers went in for the kill and bid up a storm. My favourite reproduction sold for $200—four times what I had paid five years earlier. I didn't know how the German buyer was going to pick it up, but two days later a delivery guy turned up to take it away. It seemed like a lot of effort for a $200 chair, but who was I to say anything.

The $820 went straight into my super saver account, and by the beginning of the silly season it had just under $9000 with a little over a month to go.

All I had to do to get to $10 000 was control myself in the lead-up to Christmas. I had settled so well into the budget, mainly because I liked the structure and as a journalist I work well with deadlines, but now it was time to finish what I had started.

I had no idea what I was going to get people as gifts on the cheap. My parents were certainly going to have to forgo any expensive presents like the Tivoli radio I had given them the year before and Spencer was going to have to wait for his next birthday for a really special gift. The thing was, though, I had a lot of money in the bank and it seemed pretty lame to be stingy at Christmas just so I could get to the $10 000 goal a few weeks later. There had to be a way around this Christmas gift-giving drama to keep everyone happy.

I talked to Spencer and we agreed we would forgo presents for our first Christmas together and celebrate when I reached my goal. We had planned to go to the beach for a week in mid-January and I planned to indulge in good wine, good food and a good man.

I went through my budget with a fine toothcomb to see where I could cut back in the few weeks before Christmas and buy my parents something nice. It was tight as it was and I was in the zone with the numbers I had, but Jason had told me once in a meeting that people's spending contracted and expanded along with their pay packets and there was always room for penny pinching. After much staring at the spreadsheet I decided I was going to spend a maximum of $250.

The money bought my mum concert tickets to the Waltzing Maestros, a lame German violin troupe my mother, and every other woman over 60, seemed to have developed a mad crush on. My dad and my brothers were not going to be swayed by the music troupe, so I had to come up with something else to make them happy. As a journalist I had reciprocal staff benefits at a bookshop in town. This gave me 20 per cent off any nonsale item in the store. I spent an hour walking the aisles before I was happy with the books I had chosen. When all else fails a book never does.

The Saturday before Christmas I was home alone pottering around the house thinking about how good my friends had been to me throughout the year and how different things were from 12 months earlier when I was out on the town every night spending money I didn't have. I was going to thank them and I knew exactly how I was going to do so—I was going to make apricot jam. I just knew my friends would go into shock when I handed them a perfectly preserved pot of homemade apricot conserve à la Maggie Rose.

I chose jam because (a) it would keep and (b) it was dirt cheap to make. A big batch only required one and a half kilograms of apricots, water, lemon juice and sugar. It didn't take long to cook, and then all I had to do was set it, store it and send it off. I used old jam jars Eliza and I had kept. Why did we have them? Neither of us knew the answer to that. It certainly wasn't to preserve jam. Once the jam was cooked, I signed, sealed and delivered each pot to Fran, Tim, Max, Jem, Genevieve, Spencer, Eliza and Tom. No-one was more impressed with me than myself. The whole exercise cost only $25. A delicious bargain.

With the presents sorted I just had to see it through the 10 Christmas parties I had been invited to. I said no to the two dinners I had attended the year before and had spent a truckload of money at, and chose to go only to the places where food and drinks were gratis—as a good Christmas shindig should be. The one dinner I did decide to go to where I had to pay was with a whole lot of journalists. It was an annual dinner and was being held at Concord's where Eliza had celebrated her birthday in January. I couldn't resist a chance to tuck into the food again and Spencer was coming along to keep me in line. I didn't need his help, though, as our editor was sitting next to us and if there was ever a reason to eat and run this was it, but she wanted to talk shop.

She started discussing the O'Brien scandal and how well it had gone for the paper. She said newspapers had flown off the shelves that week. She was nice, much more normal than Janice, and was actually interested in what I wanted to do. I said I was happy in the newsroom, but would really like to get into writing a blog or a column — wink-wink, nudge-nudge. I didn't think it would get me anywhere, but it never hurts to tell people what you want.

Since the O'Brien scandal things at work had settled down. It could have just been the year winding to a close or it might have just been a return to the norm after a hectic 12 months, but the world seemed like a much quieter and more content place. I was happy writing about what the good citizens had done over Christmas and I was willing to go back to the beach again and watch the teenagers enjoy their seemingly endless freedom.

Fortunately, Janice showed me I had earned her respect in the kindest possible way and gave me New Year's Eve off. I was no longer a junior journo, and as I was leaving the office to head off into the afternoon to celebrate with my friends she grabbed me for a quick end-of-year chat.

'It's been a good year, Maggie. Do you have time for a quick talk?'

The woman had impeccable timing. She had persecuted me from day one and although she had somewhat explained herself, it in no way meant I wanted to sit down and get into a deep and meaningful with her on the last day of the year.

'I'm glad it's over. I'm ready for a fresh start', I said.

'I know you probably want to get home. I just wanted to let you know there's going to be a bit of reshuffling across the newspaper in the coming weeks and I thought you should know I plan to move you around a bit more.'

I wanted to scream with delight, but I had to hear where I was being sent first. I still didn't trust the woman and for all I knew she could have paired me with Dave or had me on permanent stake-out somewhere.

'Where am I going?' I asked tentatively.

'Dave is leaving the paper and you will be moved into his role on crime.'

'Why is Dave leaving?' I asked in disbelief.

'Between you and me, he got a little drunk at a Christmas party and flashed the editor. For some reason he didn't recognise her when he went in for the kill and tried to chat her up. Needless to say, he's not welcome back in the office', she regaled.

I couldn't believe it. Karma is a wonderful thing.

'As far as your new position goes, you'll be doing mostly breaking news, but the editor has requested you also write a lifestyle blog once a week for the website. Is that something you would be interested in?'

It was perfect. It may not have been a full-time column, but who was I to complain when I would have an actual role, a blog and creepy Dave was gone. Thank God I was seated next to the editor at that Christmas party.

'Does it include a pay rise?' I asked. I wasn't going to feel bad about talking about money. It had been a big year, I had brought in the O'Brien scoop and what was I, a martyr?

'Yes, but we'll discuss that later.'

Sweet Janice had saved my skin. I walked home and, using my $50 alcohol budget, bought the best bottle of champagne it would buy to ring in the new year.

On 12 January, my final day at work before Spencer and I went to the beach, I walked into the office, logged onto my computer and opened my super saver account. It was my first day in the new job and I had been too busy to check my balance. In fact, I hadn't checked it since Boxing Day when I had managed to get through Christmas unscathed.

And there it was. A grand total of $9589.78. I logged out of my super saver page and went straight into my regular savings account, clicked on the transfer button and moved the $800 annual leave pay that had been deposited two days before into the super saver account, increasing my balance to $10 389.78. I'd done it.

It was time to celebrate, and I knew exactly how I was going to reward myself—a blow-wave. I may have been going to the beach the next day but I didn't care. As I meandered home from the hairdressers, with my lush, perfectly dried locks, I thought about where I was 12 months earlier. Sitting in a car, broke, unhappy and on the verge of eviction. I knew my life could have been a hell of a lot worse and I was not in a position to bemoan a situation I had created myself, but it didn't change the fact that I had been a seriously unhappy woman.

So after spending a year living thin, countless mistakes, several financial crises and with a little bit of help from my friends, I had done it—I had changed my life. And just as I hoped, I felt like a happier, lighter and more fulfilled human being. I could finally look to the future and start planning for things I would never have dreamed were within my grasp 12 months earlier. Not only had I saved $10 000, but I had also showed myself I was capable of putting me first, and that was the biggest achievement of all.

Debt: $0
Savings: $10 389.78
Happiness: delirious!

Lessons learned

- Catching up with friends doesn't have to involve going out and spending big — visiting each other's houses and taking turns to make dinner is both a lot of fun and cheap.

- Watching your money grow is addictive and a great way to keep you focused on your savings goal.

- Tequila shots are never a good idea ...

- To avoid any scary mobile phone bills, when travelling overseas make sure the internet roaming function on your phone is turned off and keep calls as brief as possible.

- Selling your stuff on eBay can help you make some quick cash.

- Work out how much you can afford to spend at Christmas and stay within your budget. Home-made gifts are always a winner.

Maggie's top 10 saving tips

In the year I spent living thin, through trial and error I learned many things about getting out of debt and saving. Now that you've discovered what to do — and, perhaps more importantly, what not to do! — here are my top 10 tips:

* Take control of your own finances — know exactly how much money you have coming in and where it is all going.

* Get yourself out of debt before worrying about saving. There's not much point having $10 000 in the bank if you have $5000 in debt. Do yourself a favour and get rid of it.

* Set up a high-interest savings account that is separate from your everyday savings account. Even if you're only making an extra $100 a year in interest, it's better than the money sitting in your everyday savings account, where the interest is next to nothing.

✱ Pay yourself first—that is, set aside an amount of money from each pay cheque to go into your high-interest savings account. This is Jason's money mantra and is an essential step in getting ahead.

✱ Be credit card savvy—know how much interest you are paying on your cards and try to keep only one card for emergency purchases such as your car breaking down or washing machine dying, not when you spot an amazing Prada bag at 40 per cent off.

✱ Shop around, and negotiate, when making essential expensive purchases. There is always a better offer.

✱ Be realistic about what you can and can't afford. Can you really afford to get your hair cut and coloured every six to eight weeks? Be ruthless—cut back on expenses that aren't essential.

✱ Prepare a weekly and monthly budget so you can see where your money is supposed to go. Even if you fall off the rails trying to stick to it, preparing a budget will make you think about your finances. Don't be too hard on yourself if you do slip up, just be sure to make up for it.

✱ Get up a little earlier and have breakfast at home (or even take it to work) and make your lunch.

✱ If you can, walk to work. This will save you money, help you keep fit and keep you focused on your savings goal.

The basic budget

If you're serious about getting rid of your debt and building up your savings, unless you have some sort of photographic maths memory, you're going to have to draw up a budget. Following is a basic guide to getting started, and I've included a sample budget on page 191:

✳ Keep track of your spending for a month to see where all your money is going.

✳ Write a list of all your essential weekly, monthly and yearly expenditures so you have a good idea what you need to spend you money on. These needs include food, rent, mortgage, debts, car registration, phone bill, utility bills, insurance, clothes and shoes.

✳ Plan ahead for your bills. Make a note of when they are due so you can put money aside for them.

✳ Write down how much you spend on discretionary items, such as entertainment, alcohol and eating

out, and work out how much you actually need
to spend.

✱ Study your bank statements, and collect and
go through all your receipts, to see what you're
spending your money on. You'll probably
be surprised by how much you spend on
miscellaneous items.

✱ Look over your pay cheque to find out exactly how
much you're earning and being taxed.

✱ Draw up a three-tiered budget so you can see
where your money is going on a weekly, monthly
and yearly basis. Jason's advice to pay yourself first
should be at the top of the list, so you can see how
much you're going to save.

✱ Do the maths and work out how much you are
going to need to spend each week to survive.
Be realistic.

✱ Subtract the amount you are going to need from
your monthly and annual income and see if the
numbers add up.

✱ If the numbers don't add up, you'll need to look
at what you are spending and work out what can
go. This is when shopping around for cheaper
insurance and being vigilant with what you need for
food and entertainment is essential.

✱ Stick to your budget and review it regularly.

Sample budget

Your income

	Weekly	Monthly	Annual
Salary			
Less tax and student loan repayment			

Your expenses

	Weekly	Monthly	Annual
Savings — pay yourself first			
Rent or mortgage			
Health insurance			
Home insurance			
Mobile phone			
Internet			
Public transport			
Groceries			
Eating out			
Alcohol			
TOTAL			
Surplus			

Maggie's guide to selling
your stuff on eBay

eBay is a great way to both make some extra cash and get rid of preloved belongings hanging around the house. Whether you want to sell clothes, shoes, bags, books, art, furniture, music, your grandmother's wedding dress or whitegoods, there is a market for it on eBay.

For all those eBay novices, following are some hints (adapted from *eBay For Dummies*) on how to navigate your way through the system and sell your wares, so you can make some cash and start saving just like me. eBay is set up so simply that there are prompts to get you from A to Z at every stage if you need more help.

Registering

Whether you're buying or selling you have to register. This involves filling out a registration form and creating a user identification. If you're selling your wares you must also register as a seller. You'll be asked for a bit more information, including your bank account info, and you will have to have your identification verified, but this will only take a few minutes. All information is safe and confidential.

Costs

Each item listed to sell will incur a small eBay fee called an Insertion Fee. This fee is dependant on the starting price you have set for the item you are selling. Unless you're selling very expensive items, such as cars, motorbikes, boats or other vehicles, the maximum Insertion Fee is $3.50. If the item sells, eBay also takes a small commission from the final selling price.

If you want to put a photo of your item in the eBay gallery, where it will receive a lot more attention, you will be charged an extra $0.59. When you're listing your item it will be clear which information is included in the listing fee and which is an additional cost.

Check out the website

The first step to selling on eBay is to take a look at the website <www.ebay.com.au> and research your market. Type in something in the eBay search engine you are thinking of selling and see what other people have for sale that is similar. See how many of the items you're looking to sell are already on sale, for how much and whether there is demand. Log in and then click the button that says 'Watch this item'—you can then see what the other similar items sell for and compare them to yours.

There were lots of similar beds to mine up for sale, so I knew I wasn't going to get top dollar for it, but I sold it anyway and got the price I expected, based on the other sales I'd seen.

Listing your items

So, you've registered as a seller and researched your item. The next step is to create your listing. Click the 'Sell' tab at the top right-hand side of the screen, select a category your item fits into, then describe what you're selling in the title form — be careful as you only have 55 characters to do this!

The listing form will help you to create an auction page to sell your item. It will ask you to include as much info as possible, based on the category of your item, including brand names, size, age, condition, rarity, colour and material. You'll then be asked to upload a photo of your item. The first upload is free and there are minimal costs for every one after. Finally, check over your listing and make sure it sounds (and looks) as good as it really is and sit back and watch the money roll in.

To bid or not to bid, that is the question

One critical component is deciding how you're you going to sell your item. There are three options — auction, fixed-price sale or 'Buy it now' set price. If you chose an auction, think carefully about the minimum starting price you set. If you're worried that your item is only going to sell for the minimum bid (your starting price) of $0.50, and you know it's worth much more, there are ways and means to change your auction mid-auction. You must also choose how long the auction will run for. If you're like me and desperate for some quick cash, you can set your auction for as short as one day. However, if you're willing to wait a bit longer and get more viewers, there are also three-, five-, seven- and 10-day options.

The second option is a fixed-price sale. Just as the name suggests, you name your price and hope someone comes to the party and pays.

The third option is to include a 'Buy it now' price within the auction. This allows a buyer to pay for the bookcase you're selling before the auction is over at the price you are willing to part with it for. There are some other terms and conditions associated with this type of sale, which the website will make clear to you.

Payment

You also have to decide how you want to get paid. There are several payment methods to choose from, but most people use the PayPal option. PayPal is a safe, free payment service that allows money to be transferred into your account without revealing your account details. Anyone with an email address can set up a PayPal account.

When your auction is over, click on the send information button next to the winning bidder's name so you can get paid via your preferred method. Always make sure money is received (for example, the cheque has cleared) before sending your item.

Postage and shipping

You'll need to select a postage and shipping option on your listing page. The buyer usually pays for postage and handling, so it's up to you to work out how much it's going to cost to post your item and add it to the listing. Research it thoroughly so that you don't end up paying to send the item! Also add a small amount for packaging costs. Remember, if you're sending something internationally, you have to fill out a customs form and there will be extra costs incurred. You may also have to consider insurance.

There are three postage and shipping options to choose from—within your country only, worldwide shipping and 'Will not post/Local pick-up only'. If, like me, you're selling a sizeable piece of furniture, you should elect to have the new owner pick it up from your home. But if you are selling a concert ticket, don't be a cheapskate and post the item!

If you choose to send your wares anywhere in the world, your listing will appear on all eBay websites around the globe. Just make sure to include the costs of shipping in your listing or you will end up paying to ship your piano to Denmark.

Always ask a buyer to confirm all their details so you know where to send the item. Keep a record of all your correspondence and print a copy of the final auction page with the winning bid just in case something goes wrong with the delivery.

eBay etiquette

During the auction people may ask you questions, so be sure to check your listing regularly and respond quickly. You can update your listing at any point if you realise that you have been unclear or need to add more info. When an auction finishes, make sure you congratulate the winning bidder and try to make the payment and postage or pick-up process as easy as possible for them.

As I mentioned earlier, this is just a basic guide devised to give you an idea of how to get started; the rest is up to you. Good luck!

Maggie's favourite reads

Following are some fantastic books (a number of which I read when I was trying to get control of my finances) to help out anyone struggling with debt and trying to save.

$0 to Rich by Tracey Edwards (Wrightbooks, 2008).

This is one of the best guides to sorting out your finances. Edwards teaches you to set financial goals and not only gets you on the right path towards financial security, but shows you what to do with your money once you have it. It includes terrific advice on how to pay off your credit cards and loans.

Not Buying It: My Year Without Shopping by Judith Levine (Pocket Books, 2007).

If you've ever thought about throwing in the towel and giving up on the consumer rat race, this is the book for you. Levine's hilarious and thoughtful documentation of her year without shopping makes frugal living look almost romantic.

Debt Man Walking by Bruce Brammall (Wrightbooks, 2009).

This is a serious book for gen Xers ready to take the next step into the big, bad world of investments. Brammall wittily intertwines the generation's favourite nostalgia with a step-by-step guide to getting ahead. This is not the book for you if you are just starting out on your savings journey or didn't know Julia Roberts before *Ocean's Eleven*.

Where's My Money? by Jason Cunningham (Wrightbooks, 2009).

Whether you earn $35 000 or $1 million a year, this book will help you become debt free, save, invest and fast-track your financial goals. Cunningham, the financial adviser who helped me get out of debt and save, has cleverly included several case studies so the book has wide-ranging appeal and teaches the reader to never give up.

The Barefoot Investor by Scott Pape (Pluto Press, 2007).

This book is for anyone looking for a way to achieve financial freedom regardless of income. Whether you're trying to save for your first home or your first trip overseas, Pape has great advice on how to increase your personal wealth.

Maggie's favourite websites

There are heaps of great websites that provide information on budgeting and saving, and that compare credit cards, loans, insurance and so on. Here are some of the consumer information websites I found particularly useful:

InfoChoice <www.infochoice.com.au>

Whether you're on the hunt for a home loan, savings account or personal loan this is the website to visit to compare and save.

FIDO <www.fido.gov.au>

FIDO is the Australian Securities & Investments Commission's finance and safety check website. It is one of the most comprehensive sites dedicated to personal finance and has a great budget planner.

Moneygirl <http://moneygirl.com.au/>

A smart female-orientated website with excellent information on everything to do with money. It has budgeting and saving advice, as well as more complex information on managing funds, investments and superannuation.

Credit Cards Australia <http://australia.creditcards. com>

This website reviews and rates credit cards based on a range of categories. It lists the top 10 cards, low interest cards and the best card to get if you want to transfer a balance from another card or reduce your annual fee.

The Practice <www.thepractice.com.au>

This is the homepage of Jason's company, The Practice. Check it out for information on wealth management and tax for individuals and businesses.

Once you've started building up your savings and can afford to add to your wardrobe, make sure you check the following websites to find out where you can pick up a designer bargain:

Missy Confidential <www.missyconfidential.com.au>

The latest and greatest designer fashion sales information for the savvy shopper.

Vogue forums <http://forums.vogue.com.au>

The ultimate fashion forum for women, who want to be ahead of the pack when it comes to fashion and beauty.

Maggie's tried-and-true tagliatelle with salmon and rocket

This is the quick, cheap and easy pasta dish I made for Spencer five dates in a row (adapted from Jill Dupleix's recipe in *Lighten Up*). What is great about it is you're likely to already have some of the ingredients, and others that you'll have to buy can be used again whether in this dish or another. I'll take a giant leap of faith and assume you have salt, pepper and olive oil in your cupboards, and all the other ingredients should cost you $10 to $15. Feel free to swap the tagliatelle for spaghetti or any other pasta you like. Salmon will vary in price, but at the most it should be about $29.00 per kilogram, which means you would be paying about $5.80 for 200 grams. This recipe serves two.

Ingredients

200 g salmon fillet (or 250 g tinned salmon — dolphin friendly, of course!)

2 ripe tomatoes

150 g dried tagliatelle

1.5 tbsp extra virgin olive oil

grated zest of one lemon

¼ of a red onion, sliced

juice of half a lemon

handful of rocket (or baby spinach)

salt and pepper

Method

Put the pasta on to cook, following the instructions on the packet.

While the pasta is cooking, skin the salmon (or get the fishmonger to do this for you) and chop into small cubes.

Cut the tomatoes in half, squeeze out the seeds, then cut into small chunks.

Combine the olive oil, lemon zest, and salt and pepper in a large frying pan.

When the oil is hot, add the salmon and cook gently without 'frying' until it turns pink. Add the lemon juice, tomatoes, onion and rocket and stir through.

Drain the pasta, add to the pan and gently toss, and voila, dinner is served! (If you're not afraid of carbs, and have a spare $5, serve the dish with crusty fresh bread. Mmmm…!)

Maggie's apricot jam

This is a delicious apricot jam recipe, and makes enough for five or six medium jars.

Ingredients

1.5 kg apricots (in season in summer months)

1 cup water

15 g unsalted butter

juice of 1 lemon

1.5 kg sugar

Method

Preheat the oven to 160 degrees celcius.

Wash the apricots. Halve or quarter them and remove the stones. Wrap half the stones in a tea towel and crack them with a nutcracker or mallet. Remove the kernels and set aside. (The kernels are like soft almonds and are totally yum!)

Put apricot halves and kernels, water and lemon juice into a saucepan and slowly bring to the boil. Reduce heat and vigorously simmer fruit until tender, about 15 to 20 minutes. The longer it simmers the less chunky the jam will be, but make sure it doesn't burn! Remove from heat.

Put the sugar into a baking dish, put in the oven and warm the sugar until it is hot to touch. Don't be tempted to make this 'healthy' by adding less sugar, as this is what preserves the fruit and helps the jam to set.

Return the saucepan with the fruit mixture to the heat and add warmed sugar, stirring until the sugar has dissolved, then add butter. Boil the jam for 15 minutes or until setting stage is reached. You can test if the jam is at setting stage by putting a teaspoon of it onto a cold plate and allowing it to cool. Tip the plate — if the jam doesn't slide off, then it's ready; if it does, keep cooking.

Ladle into hot, sterilised jars, taking care to distribute the kernels evenly, and seal with waxed paper discs under the lids.

The jam can be stored in the fridge for months.